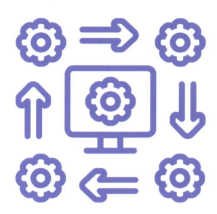

World of Workflows

User Guide

Version 1.6

August 2023

©2023 TribeTech Pty Ltd. All Rights Reserved.

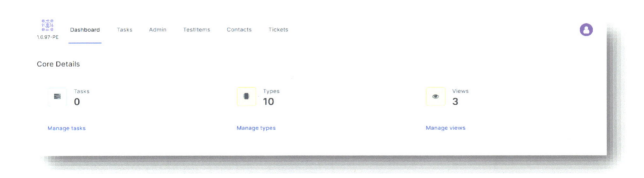

Table of Contents

Introduction

Welcome to the World of Workflows User Guide! This comprehensive manual is designed to help you understand and effectively use our innovative software product, "World of Workflows,". World of Workflows is a software solution that allows anyone to automate business processes, be those simple processes for yourself or processes which encompass your entire business. Whether you are new to workflow management or an experienced user, this guide will serve as a valuable resource as you explore the platform's features and functionalities.

Purpose of the guide

The purpose of this user guide is to provide you with clear, step-by-step instructions on how to use World of Workflows. In addition to explaining the software's core components, the guide will walk you through the process of creating, managing, and automating workflows, as well as leveraging the user-configurable database, advanced task management system and extend your use with views, plugins and solutions. It also contains reference information that you can refer to in the future as you extend your understanding and use of the platform.

Overview of World of Workflows

World of Workflows is a powerful software solution designed to streamline and optimize your business processes by providing an intuitive platform for creating, managing, and automating both simple and complex workflows. We consider any process you perform with more than one step to be considered a workflow. With over 100 activities to choose from, and plugins which extend this functionality, you can easily tailor workflows to suit your organization's specific needs. By integrating a rich, dynamic, user-configurable database and an advanced task management system, World of Workflows enables you to efficiently manage your projects and tasks, collaborate with your team, and track progress in real-time.

World of Workflows comes in two key editions:

- **Personal Edition** or PE runs on your local PC and is for personal use or workflow development.
- **Business Edition** or BE runs on any of the major cloud providers or your servers and offers enhanced features such as single sign on and rich permissions and access control.

Key features and components of World of Workflows

- Workflow Editor, a core component of World of Workflows, offers a flexible and user-friendly interface for building and customizing workflows. Some of the key features and components include:
  - A wide range of pre-built activities that can be easily added, edited, and connected within your workflows.
- A user-configurable database for managing data and integrating with external databases or APIs.
- A robust task management system that enables you to create, assign, and track tasks, as well as collaborate with your team members.
- Workflow templates for quickly implementing common processes and best practices.
- Advanced features such as workflow automation with triggers, third-party application integration, and the ability to create custom activities.
- Comprehensive security and permissions settings to ensure data protection and controlled access *with business edition*.
- Plugins, which extend the capability of the system.
- OData access which simplifies the process of reporting and dashboarding of your data.
- Credential manager which allows you to securely connect to 3rd party APIs and systems, such as ChatGPT, Xero, Office 365 and many, many more.

Our extensible database which can be accessed from the User Interface or within workflows provides the following features:

- Extremely high performance
- Customizable tables (Types), Columns and Relationships
- Custom views to see filtered and sorted database entries.
- Flexible import
- Full Export
- Inline editing
- Sort, Filter and paging

Our detailed task system allows for the system to reach out to users and instruct them where manual tasks are required and includes the following features:

- Task Queues
- Task Details formatted with Markdown
- Update data in the database directly from a task
- Custom outcomes which branch the workflow.

We hope this user guide will empower you to fully harness the potential of World of Workflows, driving efficiency and productivity within your organization.

Examples of process automation with world of workflows.

Our customers have used world of workflows to automate a number of business processes. Here are some examples:

1. A media company uses world of workflows integrated with ChatGPT to write draft articles on incoming press releases automatically.
2. A soccer club uses world of workflows to notify coaches and managers when it is their turn to put up or take down nets on a soccer field based on the draw in an external system.
3. An independent school uses world of workflows to manage their enrolment process.
4. A managed service provider users world of workflows to correctly bill customers for their telephone voice usage.
5. A sporting club uses world of workflows to automatically generate a weekly newsletter.
6. A not-for-profit uses world of workflows to manage their grants application process.

Getting Started

This chapter will guide you through the initial steps of setting up and using World of Workflows, including system requirements, installation, account creation, and navigation of the user interface. By the end of this chapter, you will be well-prepared to begin exploring the software's features and functionalities.

System requirements

Before installing World of Workflows, ensure that your system meets the following minimum requirements:

Requirement	**World of Workflows Personal Edition**	**World of Workflows Business Edition**
Operating System	Windows 10 or better	Windows 10 1607+, macOS 10.15 (Catalina) or later, or Linux (Ubuntu 18.04 or later). Includes Windows Server 2012 and above.
Processor	Intel Core i3 or equivalent	Intel Core i3 ARM processor Apple M1, M2
Memory	4Gb RAM Recommended	8Gb RAM Recommended
Disk Space	512Mb Available Storage	2Gb Available Storage
Internet Connection	Broadband Connection	Broadband Connection
Database	Included	Included or Microsoft SQL Server (Optional)

Please note that better performance may be achieved with higher system specifications.

Installation process

Installing World of Workflows PE

To install World of Workflows PE for Windows, follow the steps below:

1. Visit the World of Workflows website (www.worldofworkflows.com) and navigate to the Plans and Pricing section.
2. Choose the appropriate plan and then download the appropriate installer for your operating system (Windows, macOS, or Linux).
3. Download the installer and save it to your desired location.

4. Run the installer and follow the on-screen prompts to complete the installation process.
5. Once the installation is complete, launch World of Workflows using the desktop shortcut or by searching for it in your applications menu.

Installing World of Workflows Business

As World of Workflows Business works with Azure Active Directory, the process for installation is a little more complex and requires additional work.

Pre-requisites

In order to install world of workflows BE, you will need:

1. Access to an Azure Active Directory Account and have the "Manage Applications" permission.
2. Access to the Microsoft Azure Portal and have access to application registrations and enterprise applications
3. Access to a server to run World of Workflows. This can be Windows, Linux or Mac, will need to have a SSL certificate and be available on the web on port 443 for SSL.

Installation Process

1. Download World of Workflows BE
   a. Once you have subscribed to World of Workflows BE, you will be granted access to the installation resources. Download your copy of World of Workflows BE for the platform you are installing to. The download will come as a zip file.
2. Prepare Azure Active Directory
   a. The process to install World of Workflows BE is complicated, but has been simplified for you through a simple powershell script.
   b. Inside the zip file downloaded in section 1, above, you will find the file WOWFBEConfiguration.PS1
   c. From a powershell prompt, run as Administrator, run WOWFBEConfiguration.PS1
   d. The script will launch a browser for you to login as the admin account from the pre-requisites

   ```
   World of Workflows Business Edition Configuration Tool
   Connecting to MS Graph
   Welcome To Microsoft Graph!
   Creating Client Application in AAD
   Enter the Client Application Name [World of Workflows Client]: |
   ```

   e. the script will as for the name of the Client and Server Applications. These are for their registrations in Azure AD. Press Enter to accept the defaults or Enter your own entries. **Note:** The system creates two application registrations, one for the Client application and another for the server.

f.
```
World of Workflows Business Edition Configuration Tool
Connecting to MS Graph
Welcome To Microsoft Graph!
Creating Client Application in AAD
Enter the Client Application Name [World of Workflows Client]: WOWF Client
Enter the Server Application Name [World of Workflows Server]: WOWF Server
Enter the Base Address of your instance [https://localhost:7063]: |
```

Next, enter the address of your instance in the format as shown. This will be the final URL of your World of Workflows Installation.

g.
```
World of Workflows Business Edition Configuration Tool
Connecting to MS Graph
Welcome To Microsoft Graph!
Creating Client Application in AAD
Enter the Client Application Name [World of Workflows Client]: WOWF Client
Enter the Server Application Name [World of Workflows Server]: WOWF Server
Enter the Base Address of your instance [https://localhost:7063]:
https://localhost:7063/authentication/login-callback https://localhost:7063/swagger/oauth-redirect.html
Client Application Completed with Id:  + 8042c499-b1db-4bc3-a510-3cafabcc71dc
Now Building Server Application
Now Establishing API Scopes. Please wait...
Pre-Authorizing Client...
```

When complete, the powershell script will return you to the login prompt.

h. Navigate to App Registrations in the Azure Portal (https://portal.azure.com) -> Azure Active Directory -> App Registrations

i. Choose your Server Application named in step g above

j. Click **API Permissions**

k. Click **Add a permission**

Request API permissions

Select an API

Microsoft APIs   APIs my organization uses   My APIs

Commonly used Microsoft APIs

Microsoft Graph

Take advantage of the tremendous amount of data in Office 365, Enterprise Mobility + Security, and Windows 10. Access Azure AD, Excel, Intune, Outlook/Exchange, OneDrive, OneNote, SharePoint, Planner, and more through a single endpoint.

l.

Click **Microsoft Graph**

m. Choose **Delegated Permissions**

n. Search for **User.Read.All**

o. Select the checkbox and click Add Permissions

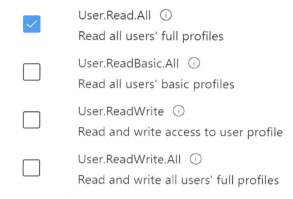

☑ User.Read.All ⓘ
Read all users' full profiles

☐ User.ReadBasic.All ⓘ
Read all users' basic profiles

☐ User.ReadWrite ⓘ
Read and write access to user profile

☐ User.ReadWrite.All ⓘ
Read and write all users' full profiles

Add permissions   Discard

p. Click **Grant Admin Consent**
q. Navigate to **Azure Active Directory -> Enterprise Applications**
r. Click the **X** on the filter saying Application type == Enterprise Applications X

View, filter, and search applications in your organization that are set up to use your Azure AD tenant as their Identity Provider.

The list of applications that are maintained by your organization are in application registrations.

| 🔍 Search by application name or object ID | Application type == **Enterprise Applications** ✕ | Application ID starts |

16 applications found

Name	↑↓	Object ID	Application ID	Homepage URL	Created on
MD MOD Demo Platf		03e89828-2204-45bf-b	aff75787-e598-43f9-a0e		6/1/2023

s. Select your Server Application
t. Click Users and Groups
u. Grant the users who will administer World of Workflows Administrative Access

Installation of Business Edition

Installation on a Windows Server using IIS

This is the procedure to install on a Windows Server using IIS

1. Create a new folder for World of Workflows
2. Extract the contents of the downloaded Zip File
3. Copy the appsettings.json file created above to that folder
4. In IIS, create a new WebSite, and point it at the folder
5. Download and install the ASP.NET Core Runtime Hosting bundle from https://dotnet.microsoft.com/en-us/download/dotnet/7.0

Installation on an Azure Web Application

The process for installation on an Azure Web Application.

1. Create a New Azure Web Application
2. Create a zip file with the root being the platform level (.e.g linux-x64)
3. Copy appsettings.json configured above to the zip file
4. In powershell, run the following commands:

```
connect-AzAccount #Connect to Azure
get-AzSubscription #Show Azure Subscriptions
set-azContext -Subscription <SubscriptionID> #Connect to the
correct subscription
publish-AzWebApp -ResourceGroupName <ResourceGroup> -Name <AppName>
-ArchivePath <Path_to_Zip_File> #publish the application
```

Navigating the user interface

The World of Workflows user interface is designed to be intuitive and user-friendly. Here are the main components to familiarize yourself with:

- **DASHBOARD:** The Dashboard provides a high-level overview of your projects, tasks, and workflows. From here, you can access the Task Management System, User Configurable Database, and Workflows editor.
- **TASKS:** This section allows you to create, assign, and manage tasks, as well as collaborate with your team.
- **VIEWS:** Views you have created will show as menu options, beside Tasks
- **ADMIN**: Accessible through the admin section in the top-right corner, this section allows you to manage
    - **WORKFLOWS**: This is where you can create, edit, and manage your workflows, add and configure activities, and automate processes using triggers.
    - **TYPES**: Here you can create, modify, and manage your data tables, export data, and integrate with external databases or APIs.
    - **VIEWS**: You can create, modify and manage collections of data types, called Views.
    - **TASKS**: You can view and manage all of the tasks in the system.
    - **IMPORT**: Our intuitive import wizard allows you to import CSV data into the platform
    - **WORKFLOWS UNIVERSITY**: Integrated training and solution content to help you get the most out of the platform
    - **DOCUMENTOR**: Instantly create automatic documentation of your configuration including database and workflows.
    - **SETTINGS**: your account settings, security, and permissions.
    - **PLUGINS**: Extend your system with plugins from our plugin library
    - **SOLUTIONS**: Import and export entire configurations to allow rapid prototyping and deployment.

With your World of Workflows account set up and a basic understanding of the user interface, you are now ready to dive into the powerful features and functionalities of the software. The following chapters will provide in-depth guidance on using the User Configurable Database, Task Management System, and Workflows to optimize your business processes.

Database

The User Configurable Database in World of Workflows is designed to help you manage your data efficiently and effectively. This chapter will provide an overview of the database functionality and guide you through the process of creating and managing tables, importing and exporting data, searching and filtering records, and integrating with external databases or APIs.

Overview of the database functionality

The User Configurable Database offers a flexible and intuitive platform for managing your data, allowing you to:

- Create custom *Types* (tables) with user-defined fields, data types, and relationships.
- Import and export data in various formats, such as CSV
- Search, filter, and sort records to quickly find the information you need.
- Integrate with external databases and APIs for seamless data synchronization and access.
- Use the database directly within workflows and tasks

Creating and managing tables

To create a new *Type* (table) in the User Configurable Database, follow these steps:

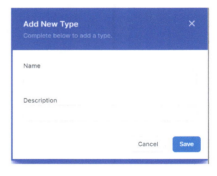

1. Navigate to the User Configurable Database section in World of Workflows, by going to *Admin* then *Types*
2. Click on the **ADD TYPES** button.
3. Enter a name for the table and a brief description (optional).
4. Click **SAVE** to confirm.

Once your *Type* is created, you can begin adding fields:

1. In the list of types, identify the type or table you want to work with.
2. Click **COLUMNS**
3. Click on the **ADD COLUMN** button.

4. Enter a name for the field and choose the Name, Display Name, Column Description and an appropriate data type (e.g., text, number, date, etc.).
5. Configure additional field properties, such as display order, visible and indexed.
6. Click "Save" to confirm.

To manage existing tables, you can:

*   Edit table names, descriptions, and field properties by clicking on the corresponding **EDIT** button.
*   Delete tables or fields by clicking on the **DELETE** button (be cautious, as this action is irreversible and is designed to work only if you don't have any entries for this *Type*).

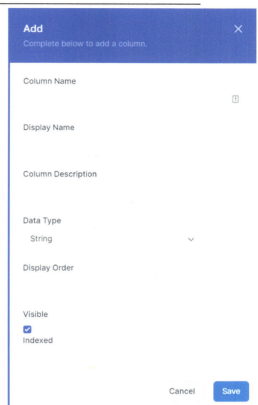

A word about data types

Every time you create a column, it needs to have a data type. This tells world of workflows how to display the data and is efficient in how the data is stored by the database. The list of available data types is below:

Name	Description	Example Uses
Big Integer	The Big Integer represents an arbitrarily large integer whose value *in theory* has no upper or lower bounds. Integers are whole numbers, positive or negative.	Commonly used as Id's for items where they may grow large, this is the type used as the Id for every object in the system.
Integer	Whole number, positive or negative.	The integer is a whole number which commonly is used to represent a count of objects, e.g. 3 people or 5 cats.
Decimal 2	Number with two decimal places.	This is a number with two decimal places,

Name	Description	Example Uses
		commonly used to represent currency
Decimal 5	Number with five decimal places	This is commonly used to represent the results of calculations, or distance
True/False	The Boolean or Bit Type	This is used to represent where we have a state that can be true/false, yes/no or off/on.
String	A collection of characters	The string can store words, sentences, paragraphs, books or any other data stored as Base64Encoded.
DateTime	The Date and Time	Used to store instances in time, this is stored in the system as UTC[1] and is presented in the system in local time.
Url	Uniform Resource Locator	This is a web link
Embed	Embed Code	Not currently used, this is a string which gets rendered in the page as an embed code.

Relationships

You can create relationships between types in World of Workflows. You do this by adding a column with the data type **Relationship** and choosing the type you would like to relate to.

Relationships allow you to define how objects are related to each other.

However, World of Workflows offers a single way to create relationships, but you can implement the three types of relationship by following the guide below:

Imagine we have Object A and Object B

- A one to one (1:1) relationship is easily established by adding a column in Object A with data type Relationship and Type the type of Object B.
- A one to many (1:∞) relationship between A and B is established by adding a column in Object B with data type relationship and Type the type of Object A

---

[1] Coordinated Universal Time or UTC is the primary time standard by which the world regulates clocks and time.

- A many to many (∞:∞) relationship between object A and B is created by creating a new type (Type C). This has two columns, one is a relationship with the type of Object A and the other is a relationship with the type of Object B.

Whilst the first two types will appear in the interface, the interface does not understand many to many relationships, however it is possible to develop a workflow that understands this structure.

Editing Columns

To edit a column, Navigate to the type itself by going to *Admin* then *Types* and then clicking the type.

You can then click *Columns* to see the list of columns and click *edit* to edit each one.

Deleting Types

If you navigate to *Admin* then *Types* you can click **Delete** to delete a type. *Note: this only works if there are no data instances in the type.*

Clicking **Delete** will immediately delete the type. If you have done this in error, you can easily recreate the type.

Editing Data

World of Workflows offers sorting, filtering, inline editing and bulk editing of your data. These features make it incredibly simple to manipulate your data in the system endure you have the correct data ready to work with.

Clicking on *Admin* then *Types* then clicking the name of the type you want to work with takes you to the data editing screen

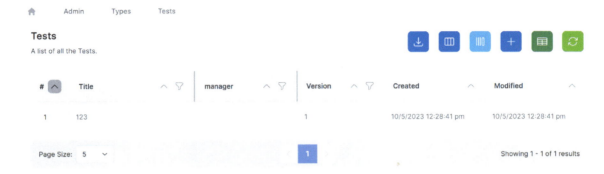

This screen allows you to manipulate your data as follows:

Columns

Columns are able to be resized and reordered. You can resize columns by hovering over the vertical separator between the column headers, clicking and dragging left and right.

Columns can be re-ordered by clicking a column header and dragging it to a new location.

Sort and Filter

To sort your data by a column, click the ∧ icon in the column header. When sorted the ∧ icon in the column header will be highlighted as shown below:

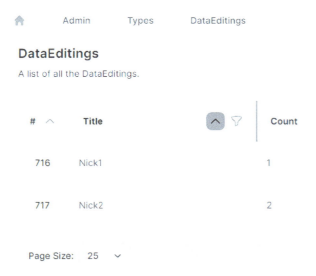

To filter your data, click the ▽ icon in any column header. This will bring up the filter window.

Either type into the filter window or click the null or not-null radio buttons to create your filter.

When a column is filtered, the filter button will be shown as highlighted

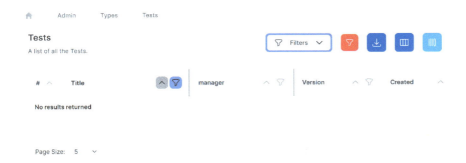

To clear all filters, click the [filter icon] button on the top of the data table, and to edit filters, click the Filters dropdown at the top of the table.

Export

To export your data, click the [download icon] button on the top of the data table. Your browser will automatically download a CSV of that data.

Add Columns

To add a column, click the [columns icon] button on top of the data table. You will see the same interface as in add column, above.

Edit Columns

To edit columns, click the [edit columns icon] button on top of the data table. You will then be navigated to the column editing screen.

Test - Columns
A list of all the properties of this Type.

Id	Name	Data Type	Display Name	Description	Order	Visible	Indexed	
1	Title	String	Title	Title of the Object	1	True	False	Edit
24	managerbeer	String	manager	manager	2	True	False	Edit Delete

Add Item

To add an item, click the [+] button. The same slide in will appear as in add an item above.

Inline edit

Clicking [inline edit icon] will change the mode to Inline Edit. From here, you can individual edit all the items.

DataEditings
A list of all the DataEditings.

	# ∧	Title		Count		
☐	716	Nick1		1		
☐	717	Nick2		2		

Page Size: 25 ∨   1   Showing 1 - 2 of 2 results

Click 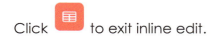 to exit inline edit.

Bulk Delete

To bulk delete, enter inline edit mode, select a number of items by clicking the

checkboxes and click the 🗑 button.

Bulk Edit

To bulk Edit, enter inline edit mode, select a number of items and click ✏. By entering data in the slide-in, you will be able to edit multiple rows at once.

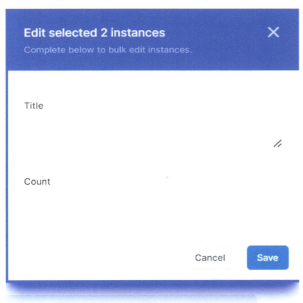

Showing 1 - 2 of 2 results

Refresh data

To refresh the data, click the 🔄 button on the top right which will reload the data for you.

To Choose number of rows shown

To choose the number of rows shown, click the page size dropdown, bottom left.

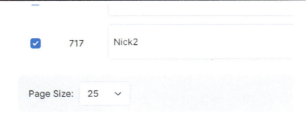

Move between pages

To move between pages, click the < or > buttons on the bottom middle of the data editor.

Importing and exporting data

World of Workflows supports data import and export in CSV.

Export

To export data, follow these steps:

1. Navigate to *Admin* -> *Types* and select the desired table.
2. Click on the ⬇ button.
3. A CSV file will shortly download.

Import

The following section describes how to import data into world of workflows.

1. Prepare a CSV with the required data and remove any columns that you do not want to import. *Column removal is not mandatory but helps speed up the process.*

2. Navigate to *Admin -> Import*

3. Click **UPLOAD A FILE** and browse to the CSV file you want to upload.

4. When you see the correct details for your CSV file, click **NEXT**.

5. If you are creating a new Type with this import, under the **TYPE** dropdown choose **NEW** and name the new type. If you are importing data to an existing

Type, select the type name in the dropdown and click **NEXT**.

6. The system will automatically suggest fields for your import. You can change these and choose:
    a. **SKIP –** This column will be ignored
    b. **NEW -** A new Column in your Type will be created in the database from the data in your CSV file. You can enter a Name, Data Type, Display Name, Description, Display Order, whether the column should be Visible and whether it will be a Title column.
    c. **<Column name>** – choose an existing column name and your CSV data will be added to this column.
    d. **ID –** This is the match to the ObjectId or Instance Id and will update records with the same Id if they exist in the database.
7. Click **NEXT** when your fields are correct

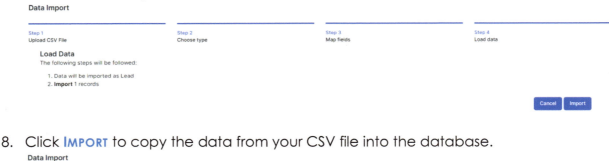

8. Click **IMPORT** to copy the data from your CSV file into the database.

Data Import

Step 1	Step 2	Step 3	Step 4
Upload CSV File	Choose type	Map fields	Load data

Load Data
Import Complete.

Views

Views are a powerful feature in World of Workflows that allow you to create customized, reusable views of your data by defining queries, selecting fields, and specifying the sorting order. With the ability to establish a hierarchy among views, you can create organized, easily accessible menu structures. This chapter will guide you through the process of creating, managing, and organizing views in the User Configurable Database.

Overview of Views

Views enable you to:

- Create custom, reusable data views based on specific queries and filters.
- Select which fields to display and customize the order in which they appear.
- Specify the sorting order for records.
- Organize views hierarchically, with top-level views appearing in the main menu and child views accessible via buttons within their parent view.

Creating a new view

To create a new view, follow these steps:

1. Navigate to **ADMIN -> VIEWS** in World of Workflows.
2. Click on the **ADD VIEW** button.

3. Enter a name and a brief description for the view (optional).
4. Choose the *Type* from which the *View* will show the data.
5. Define the fields which will be shown for the view:
    a. click the **+** next to the field name.
    b. Use the **=** handle to drag the fields to the correct order.
    c. Use the 🗑 to remove this field from the view.

6. Choose the fields to order the view by clicking the **+** next to the field name. Use the up and down arrows to select the direction of sorting.

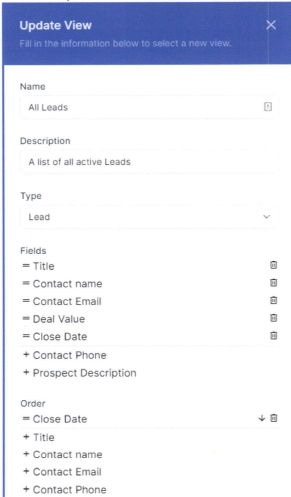

7. Create a query for the View, using *oData Query Syntax*
8. If applicable, choose a parent view from the **PARENT VIEW** dropdown menu. If no parent is selected, the view will appear in the top menu.
9. Click **CREATE VIEW** to confirm.

Managing views

To edit or delete an existing view, follow these steps:.

1. Navigate to **ADMIN** -> **VIEWS** and locate the view you want to modify or remove.
2. Click on the **EDIT** button to modify the view's settings, such as the name, description, filters, displayed fields, sorting order, or parent view.
3. Click **SAVE CHANGES** to confirm any modifications.

To delete a view, click on the **DELETE** button. Be cautious, as this action is irreversible.

Organizing views with hierarchy

Views can be organized hierarchically, which allows you to create structured navigation and improve the user experience. When a view has a parent, it will appear as a button within that parent view. To create a hierarchical structure, follow these steps:

1. While creating or editing a view, select the desired parent view from the **PARENT VIEW** dropdown menu.
2. **SAVE** your changes. The view will now appear as a button within the parent view.
3. To rearrange the order of child views within a parent view, navigate to the parent view's settings and use the drag-and-drop functionality to rearrange the child views.
4. Save your changes.

By utilizing the *Views*, you can create customized, organized representations of your data, making it easier for you and your team to access and analyze essential information.

Inline Edit

When using a view, you have the same inline and bulk edit/delete features that you have with types.

Data Editor

The data editor is where you can view data, edit fields, run workflows, view tasks and examine history.

Clicking any instance of a type or in a view brings up the data editor.

View Data

The first tab is called view and here you can view all the data in an instance, and also the date it was first created, the date it was last modified and the reason for the modification.

Edit Data

The Edit data tab allows you to edit data associated with this object

Workflows

The Workflows tab allows you to run any workflow which contains the **Object Instance Trigger** activity which is associated with the type of the object you are viewing.

The **Workflows** section shows workflows you can run using this object as reference and the **Workflow Instances** section shows workflows you can resume using this object as a reference.

Tasks

Tasks can be associated with an object instance and the Tasks tab shows all of the tasks associated with this object.

History

The History tab shows all the different modifications to this object over time.

Test #1 - 123
Test

View   Edit   Workflows   Tasks   History

History
All changes to this item over time.

#	Title	Version	Modified	Modification Reason	Original Version
1		0	10-3-2023 17:28:41 pm	Initial Creation	

Tasks

The Task Management System in World of Workflows is designed to help users efficiently manage and organize the work assigned to them. _Tasks_ are created by _Workflows_ and form an important part of the automation of a business process.

This chapter will discuss how to interact with tasks, including picking tasks, understanding task details, updating database fields, and working with action buttons. The creation of tasks within workflows will be covered in a later chapter.

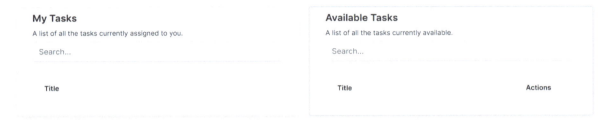

Overview of the Task Management System

The Task Management System provides the following capabilities:

- View and browse available _Tasks_ assigned to you or unassigned.
- **PICK** a _Task_, adding it to your personal to-do list.
- View _Task_ details, including the title, formatted description, and any associated data to enter into the _Task_.
- Update database details directly within a _Task_.
- Complete tasks by clicking action buttons, which correspond to different branches in the workflow.

Picking tasks

To pick a task and add it to your personal to-do list, follow these steps:

1. Navigate to **TASKS** in World of Workflows.
2. On the right hand side, you will see a list of available task..
3. To pick a task, click on the _Pick_ button next to the desired task (or click on the text in the task). The task will now appear in your personal to-do list. This step ensures that no other user will see the _Task_ and tells World of Workflows that you are now responsible for completing the _Task_.

Understanding task details

When you open a task, you will see the following information:

- _Title_: A brief, descriptive title for the task.
- _Description_: A detailed, formatted description providing instructions or context for the task.

- *Fields*: Custom fields associated with the task, which may require input or updates. Not all tasks will have custom fields: this is determined when building the *Workflow* that started the task.
- *Choices*: Buttons allow you to complete the task, or the ability to unassign the task to return it to the queue.

Updating database fields within tasks

To update the database fields within a task, follow these steps:

1. Open the *Task* by clicking on its title in your personal to-do list.
2. Locate the entry field(s) that require input or updates.
3. Enter or modify the data as necessary.
4. Click **SAVE/SUBMIT** or a similar button,-to save your changes and update the database.

Working with action buttons

Tasks may have one or more action *Buttons*, each corresponding to a different branch in the workflow. To complete a task, click on the appropriate action button:

1. Open the *Task* by clicking on its title in your personal to-do list.
2. Review the task details and ensure that all required fields have been updated.
3. Click on the action *Button* that corresponds to the desired outcome or next step in the workflow. This will mark the task as complete and trigger any subsequent actions or tasks in the workflow.

Remember that tasks are created and associated with workflows, which will be covered in more detail in a later chapter. By utilizing the Task Management System in World of Workflows, you can efficiently manage your tasks, collaborate with your team, and ensure smooth progression through your business process as defined in your workflows.

Reporting

Reporting on World of Workflows can be performed using any oData Client. Examples of this are Excel, PowerBI or Tableau. The following instructions are for Excel:

Excel

Open a new spreadsheet in Microsoft Excel

Click the **Data** menu

Click **Get Data**

Choose **From Other Sources** and choose **oData feed.**

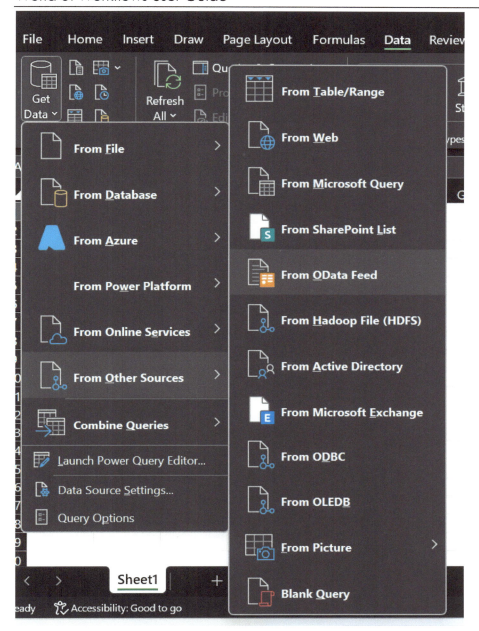

In the OData feed window, enter the URL of your World of Workflows Instance followed by /odata. For example for World of Workflows PE this will be https://localhost:7063/odata. Once done, click Ok

Next, for World of Workflows Business Edition, choose Organizational Account and Login. For World of Workflows Personal Edition, just click **Connect**

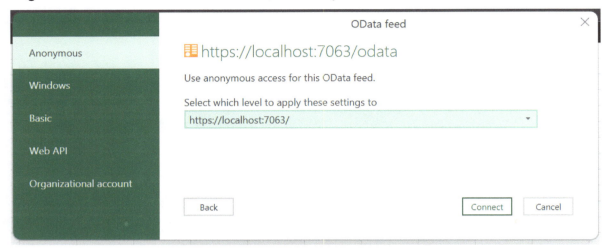

Next, select the items you want to report on. For each type there are two tables, the **CurrentState** and the **HistoryState.** Current State is the current configuration of those objects whereas History State is the history and changes for that object.

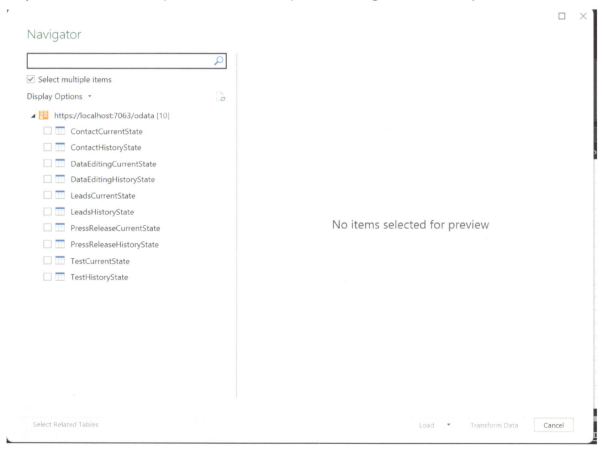

When you have selected your tables click **Transform Data.**

You will now be working with the Power Query Editor. Please refer to Excel documentation on how to manipulate this data. When complete click **Close & Load**

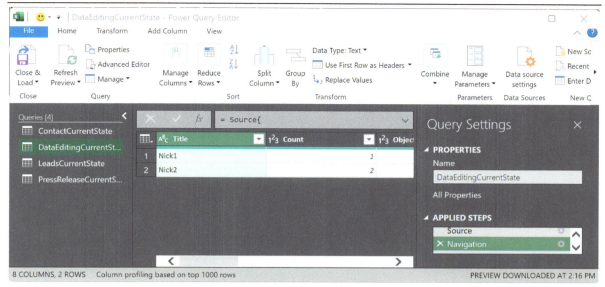

8 COLUMNS, 2 ROWS   Column profiling based on top 1000 rows   PREVIEW DOWNLOADED AT 2:16 PM

Building Workflows

Workflows, a core feature of World of Workflows, provides a powerful and intuitive platform for designing, managing, and automating your business processes. This chapter will guide you through the process of building workflows using the Workflows Editor, adding and configuring activities, and implementing triggers to automate processes.

- **WORKFLOW DEFINITIONS** are the description of what a workflow will do.
- **WORKFLOW INSTANCES** are unique instances of workflow definitions that are currently running or have finished running.
- **ACTIVITIES** are individual steps within a workflow.

Overview of Workflows

Workflows allows you to:

- Create visual, drag-and-drop workflows to model your business processes.
- Choose from over 100 activities to perform various tasks and operations.
- Configure activity settings and properties to customize workflow behaviour.
- Connect activities using transitions to define the flow of your processes.
- Implement triggers to automate workflows based on events or schedules.

Using the Workflows Editor

To create a new workflow using the Workflows Editor, follow these steps:

1. Navigate to **ADMIN -> WORKFLOWS** in World of Workflows.

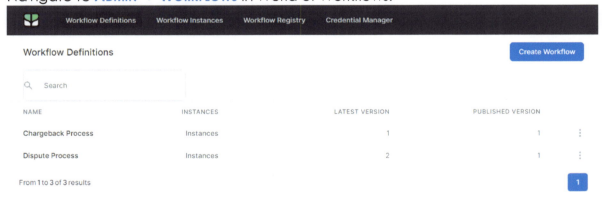

2. Click on the **CREATE WORKFLOW** button.

3. The Workflows Editor opens.

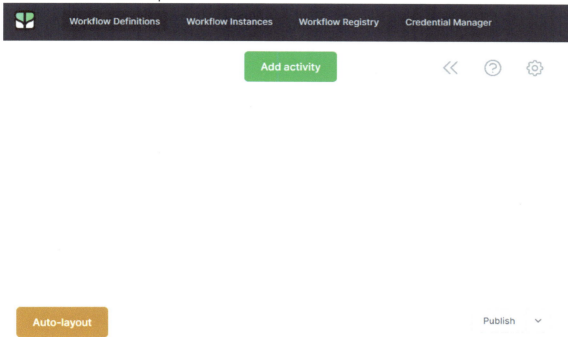

The Workflows Editor provides a visual, drag-and-drop interface for designing your workflows. You can add activities from the toolbox, connect them using transitions, and configure their properties to customize their behaviour.

Adding and configuring activities

To add an activity to your workflow, follow these steps:

1. Click **ADD ACTIVITY**. You can search for activities by name or browse through categories.

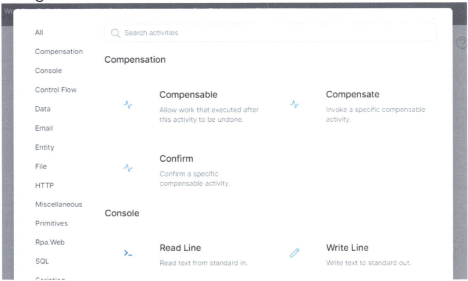

2. Click on the activity and drag it onto the canvas.
3. To configure the activity, right click the activity and choose *Edit*. Here, you can set various options, such as input and output variables, settings, and conditions.

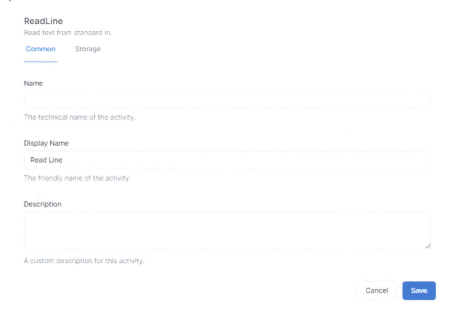

Connecting activities

Connectors define the flow of your workflow by connecting one activity to another. To create a transition, follow these steps:

1. Click on the *Connect* icon (a filled circle) at the edge of the source activity.
2. Drag the connection line to the input of the target activity (an empty circle) and release.

Implementing triggers

Triggers allow you to automate the execution of your workflows based on events, schedules, or other conditions. To add a trigger to your workflow, follow these steps:

1. In the Workflows Editor, click on the *Activities* button.
2. Find an activity that is colored red (this is a trigger).
3. Select the trigger type (e.g., timer, HTTP Endpoint, Object Instance Trigger, etc.) and configure the settings specific to that trigger type, such as the interval for a timer or the URL for a HTTP Endpoint.
4. Save your trigger.

Once you have designed your workflow, configured activities, and set up triggers, you can save and publish your workflow by clicking the PUBLISH button in the Workflows Editor. Published workflows can be executed automatically based on their triggers.

What are Workflows?

Workflows are like small processes which run in the system to complete a business process. There are many of the structures one might find in programming languages. The section below is for complete novices at programming or telling computers to do things.

Computers are machines which follow our instructions exactly. Sometimes it doesn't seem like this because modern computers are performing billions of operations every second and it is difficult to see what the instructions are.

Workflows allows you to write instructions for the computer to follow. These can include sending emails, reading data or writing and saving files. Workflows makes this simpler, by providing a simple graphical interface.

Common Settings

Every *Activity* in *Workflows* allows you to set the following:

Common Settings

Common settings are the same for every activity. They include Name, Display Name and Description and are used as follows:

- **Name**: Use this name to refer to this activity in future activities using Liquid or JavaScript.
- **Display Name** – Use this to change how the activity is named in the designer.
- **Description** – Use this to show other workflow developers how this activity is used and what it is for.

Variables

Variables are temporary places to store information. It's common to want to store information and retrieve and work with it later. With Workflows, we can define both variables and transient variables which can store all types of data and information.

Variables are created with the *Set Variable* activity. They can also be created in *JavaScript* using a *SetVariable()* command. Variables are read using a *JavaScript* command *GetVariable()* or with *Liquid* using a command such as *{{Variables.variableName}}*

Variables exist only while the workflow is running. To keep the data permanently you will need to write variable to a field in a Type.

Flow control

You will use the flow control features in Workflows to link your Activities in Workflows, and provide the logic required to formalise your business process.

This chapter will provide an overview of the core Flow Control activities, including *Break*, *For*, *For Each*, *Fork*, *If/Else*, *Join*, *Parallel For Each*, *Switch*, *While*, *Set Variable*, and *Set Transient Variable*.

JavaScript and Liquid

You can enter information into the Properties of *Activities* using either the default format (ie just typing in text, numbers or dates.

For example, here is the SetVariable activity. It asks for a *Variable Name* and a Value. You would enter the variable name as normal text.

The Value can be entered as either JavaScript, Liquid or Default text. Click on the ⊙ above the entry box to switch the type of input you need.

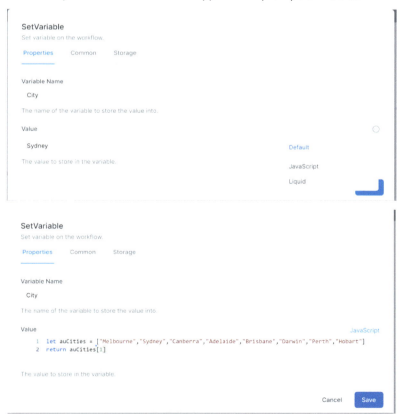

AN EXAMPLE OF SETTING A VARIABLE WITH JAVASCRIPT.

JavaScript is a powerful language which is simple to learn and provides significant extensibility to the platform.

Liquid is simpler and allows the creation of strings from other data.

Loops

We often want computers and workflows to repeat themselves. For example we might want the same process to occur for every row of a spreadsheet or every lead in a database. For this we use loops. In workflows we have a several types of loops:

For

The *For Loop* has a starting number, an ending number and a step. This loop will maintain a counter. On the first pass (iteration), the counter is set to the starting number. On the second iteration, the counter has the step value added to it. The system then compares the counter to the ending number and will only keep going if the counter is less than the ending number.

The for loop is useful when we want to count through several things where we know or can easily calculate the starting number or step.

For loops can count up (Step >0) or down (Step<0) and the comparison can be any of less than, less than or equal to, greater than and greater then or equal to.

The *For* activity requires an initial value, an end value, and an optional step value. The loop will continue to execute the activities within it until the end value is reached or a Break activity is encountered.

The For activity allows you to set the following:

- **START** – This is a number which defines the start counter for the loop. This can be entered directly into the activity or calculated using Javascript or Liquid.
- **END** – This is a number which defines the end comparison for the loop. This can be entered directly into the activity or calculated using JavaScript or Liquid.

For Each

The *For Each* activity is designed to iterate over a collection of items, such as an array or a list. It will execute the activities within the loop for each item in the collection. The loop will continue until all items have been processed or a Break activity is encountered.

Imagine we have a variable with the colors in the rainbow. We might represent it as:

```
[
    "Red",
    "Orange",
    "Yellow",
    "Green",
    "Blue",
    "Indigo",
    "Violet"
]
```

The item above is known as a **JSON array**. A *For Each loop*, using this JSON array as the Iᴛᴇᴍs, would run through seven times and return "Red", "Orange" etc until it finished with "Violet".

Parallel For Each

Workflows also has the *Parallel For each* activity which performs each iteration in parallel, increasing performance as many things happen at the same time.

The *Parallel For Each* activity is similar to the *For Each* activity. However it deals with each of the items in the collection concurrently. This can improve performance by parallelizing the processing of tasks. Just be aware of any logic problems that this may lead to.

Break

The Break activity allows you to exit a loop (e.g., *For, For Each, While*) prematurely when a certain condition is met. By implementing the *Break* activity, you can optimize your workflows and prevent unnecessary iterations.

The break activity has no need for specific customisable attributes, apart from the standard common and storage sections.

The For activity is a loop structure that iterates over a specific range of values. It requires an initial value, an end value, and an optional step value. The loop will continue to execute the activities within it until the end value is reached or a Break activity is encountered.

- The For activity allows you to set the following: **Start** – This is a number which defines the start counter for the loop. This can be entered directly into the activity or calculated using Javascript or Liquid. **End** – This is a number which defines the end comparison for the loop. This can be entered directly into the activity or calculated using Javascript or Liquid.

For EachThe For Each activity is designed to iterate over a collection of items, such as an array or a list. It will execute the activities within the loop for each item in the collection. The loop will continue until all items have been processed or a Break activity is encountered.

Fork

The Fork activity allows you to create parallel branches in your workflow, running the branches one at a time. The workflow will continue once all branches have completed.

This could be represented in a Workflow like this:

If/Else

The *If/Else* activity provides conditional branching based on a specified condition. If the condition is met, this Activity will run the TRUE branch; otherwise, the activities in the FALSE branch will be executed.

Join

The *Join* activity can be used in conjunction with the *Fork* activity to synchronize parallel branches. When parallel branches have completed their execution, the workflow will continue at the Join activity, merging the branches back into a single path.

Join has a *Mode* to perform 2 distinct types of *Join*.

> **WAITALL** will ensure that execution of the workflows will wait until all of the branches linked to the join have completed.

> **WAITANY** will continue execution of the workflow after the first branch completes. The other branches may continue execution, but the join operation will occur after just 1 branch completes.

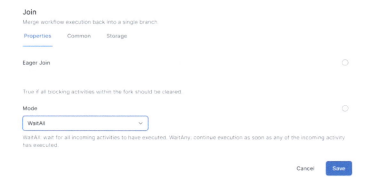

Parallel For Each

The Parallel For Each activity is similar to the For Each activity but processes items in the collection concurrently. This can improve performance by parallelizing the processing of tasks.

Switch

The *Switch* activity provides multi-way branching based on the value of a specified expression.

It allows you to define multiple cases, each with a set of activities that will be executed when the expression matches the case value.

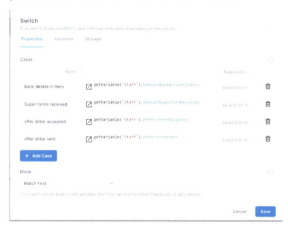

This could be represented in a *Workflow* like this:

While

The While activity is a loop structure that executes activities within the loop as long as a specified condition remains true. The loop will continue until the condition becomes false or a Break activity is encountered.

Set Variable

The *SetVariable* activity is used to create or update a variable within the workflow. It allows you to define a name and assign a value to the variable. Variables created using this activity persist throughout the entire workflow execution.

Set Transient Variable

The Set Transient Variable activity is similar to the Set Variable activity but creates variables that exist only for the current iteration of a loop. This can be useful for managing temporary data within loop structures, such as For, For Each, or While loops. Each time the loop executes the Transient Variable will be empty/null.

By using these core activities in Workflows, you can create powerful and flexible workflows that model your business processes effectively and efficiently in World of Workflows. Understanding these core activities will help you better design and optimize your workflows to meet the unique requirements of your organization.

Task Management Activities

Task Management activities in *Workflows* enable the creation, deletion, modification, and retrieval of *Tasks* within your workflows. This chapter will focus on *Task Create, Task Delete, Task Detail Create, Task Update,* and *Task Details Read* activities, with an emphasis on the core *Task Create* activity.

Task Create

The Task Create activity is the central component for creating tasks in Workflows. It allows you to configure various properties for the task, including Title, Description, Severity, Priority, Due Date, Related Object ID, Data Questions, Variable Name, and Branches.

- **Title**: The task's title, providing a brief and informative description.
- **Description**: A detailed and formatted description of the task, written in *Markdown*. *Markdown* is a lightweight markup language that allows you to create formatted text using a simple syntax. It supports formatting elements such as headings, bold, italics, lists, links, and more. For a quick guide on Markdown syntax, you can refer to this [Markdown Cheatsheet](#).
- **Severity**: A numerical value representing the task's severity or importance.
- **Priority**: A numerical value indicating the task's priority level.
- **Due Date**: The number of days from when the task is created to when the task is due.
- **Related Object ID**: A reference to a row in any *type* within the *User Configurable Database*.
- **Data Questions**: Allows you to add fields from the *Type* of the *Related Object ID* and prompt the user to complete them within the task.
- **Variable Name**: Assigns the updated row to a *Variable* for further use within the workflow.
- **Branches**: Correspond to *Buttons* in the *Task*, which can send the workflow down different branches based on the user's actions.

Task Delete

The *Task Delete* activity allows you to remove a task from the system. It requires the task's unique identifier as input and permanently deletes the specified task.

Task Detail Create

The *Task Detail Create* activity enables you to add additional information or properties to an existing task. This can be useful for providing more context, instructions, or metadata for the task. It requires the task's unique identifier as input and saves the new details to the task.

Task Update

The *Task Update* activity allows you to modify an existing task's properties, such as its TITLE, DESCRIPTION, SEVERITY, PRIORITY, DUE DATE, and RELATED OBJECT ID. It requires the *Task's* unique identifier as input and saves the updated properties to the *Task*.

Task Details Read

The *Task Details Read* activity retrieves the details of a task, including its TITLE, DESCRIPTION, SEVERITY, PRIORITY, DUE DATE, RELATED OBJECT ID, and DATA QUESTIONS. It requires the task's unique identifier as input and outputs the task details as Variables, which can be used later in the workflow.

By using these Task Management activities in Workflows, you can seamlessly integrate task-related operations into your business processes, ensuring that your team stays organized and efficient. Understanding these activities will help you better design your workflows and effectively manage tasks in World of Workflows.

HTTP Activities in Workflows

HTTP activities in Workflows enable seamless integration with external web services and APIs, as well as handling incoming HTTP requests within your workflows.

Note: While we call these HTTP activities, they almost always run over https.

This chapter will provide an overview of the three primary HTTP activities: *HTTP Endpoint, Send HTTP Request,* and *HTTP Response*, along with the *Redirect* activity.

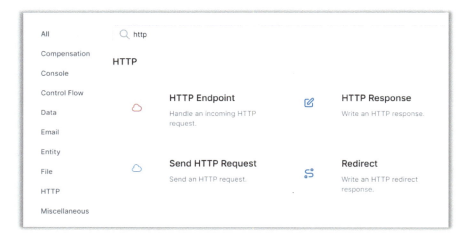

HTTP Endpoint

The *HTTP Endpoint* activity allows you to handle incoming HTTP requests within your workflow. It supports various HTTP methods, including GET, POST, PUT, DELETE, PATCH, OPTIONS, and HEAD.

Key features of the HTTP Endpoint activity include:

- **Path**: Define a custom path for the endpoint.
- **Read Content**: Choose whether or not to read the request content, and specify the format (e.g., JSON, XML, or plain text).
- **JSON Schema**: In the **ADVANCED** tab, you can define a JSON schema for validating incoming request data.
- **Security**: Secure the endpoint by enabling the **AUTHORIZE** option in the **SECURITY** tab, which restricts access to authorized users.

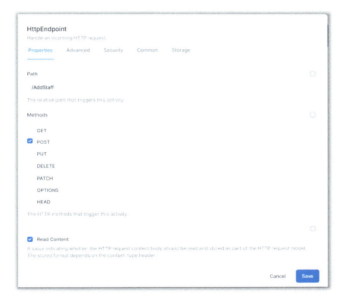

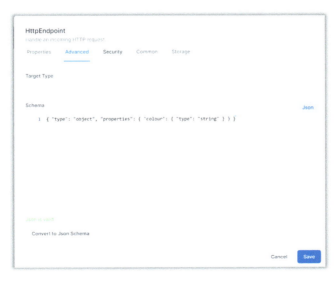

Send HTTP Request

The *Send HTTP Request* activity enables your workflows to interact with external web services and APIs by sending HTTP requests and processing the responses.

Key features of the Send HTTP Request activity include:

- **HTTP Method**: Select the desired HTTP method (e.g., GET, POST, PUT, DELETE, etc.).
- **URL**: Specify the target URL for the request.
- **Headers**: Define any custom headers to include in the request.
- **Request Body**: Provide the request body content, if applicable.
- **Authorisation**: Use CREDENTIAL MANAGER to store and manage *OAuth* and other authorization credentials for secure access to external services, then select the Authorisation here.

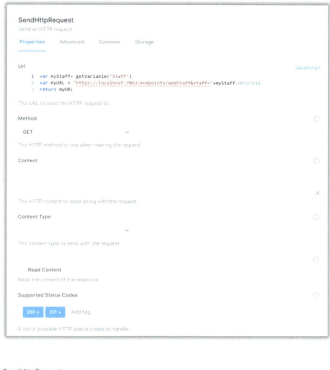

HTTP Response

The *HTTP Response* activity allows you to send an HTTP response to an HTTP Endpoint within your workflow. It provides options for customizing the response, including the status code, headers, and content.

Key features of the HTTP Response activity include:

- **Status Code**: Select the appropriate HTTP status code for the response.
- **Headers**: Define any custom headers to include in the response.
- **Content**: Provide the response content, which can be in various formats such as JSON, XML, or plain text.

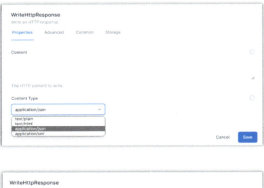

Redirect

The *Redirect* activity writes an HTTP Redirect response, allowing you to redirect the client to a different URL within your workflow. This can be useful for scenarios such as user authentication or navigation between different pages in a web application.

Key features of the Redirect activity include:

- **URL**: Specify the target URL for the redirection.
- **Permanent**: Select for the redirection to be 301 / permanent redirect, deselect for 302 / temporary redirect.

By leveraging these HTTP activities in Elsa Workflows, you can create powerful and flexible workflows that interact with external web services and APIs, as well as handle incoming HTTP requests efficiently. Understanding these HTTP activities will help you better design and optimize your workflows to meet the unique requirements of your organization in World of Workflows.

Data Activities

Data Activities in Elsa Workflows provide a powerful way to interact with the *User Configurable Database* within World of Workflows.

This chapter will cover the essential Data Activities, including **DATA TYPES READ, CREATE OBJECT INSTANCE, UPDATE OBJECT INSTANCE, GET OBJECT INSTANCE, LIST OBJECT INSTANCES, LIST OBJECT INSTANCE HISTORY, COLUMN CREATE, TYPE INDEX CREATE, TYPE CREATE, TYPE DELETE, COLUMNS READ BY TYPE, TYPES READ, TYPE INDEX DELETE, JSON DATA INSERT,** and **OBJECT INSTANCE TRIGGER**

Triggers

Object Instance Trigger

The Object Instance Trigger is designed to start or resume a workflow based on your interaction with a certain *Type* in the interface.

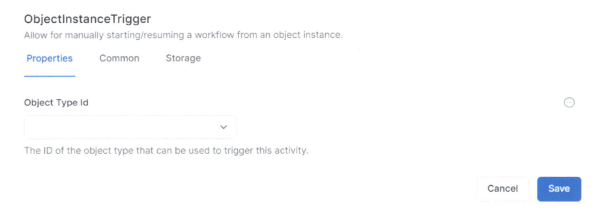

The Object Instance Trigger allows you to choose the Type you would like to initiate the workflow. It returns two variables:

1. The InstanceId of the Instance that triggered or resumed this workflow
2. The Instance itself as a well formed JSON Object

To access these variables, ensure you give this activity a name (in the Common tab)

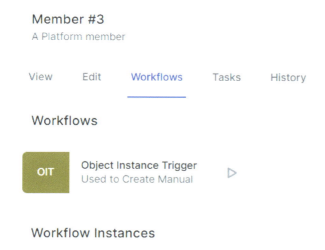

Once you have created a workflow with an Object Instance Trigger, it appears in the Object Editor under the Workflows tab.

Database Structure

As discussed in Database, the user interface in World of Workflow allows you to set up your database structure. For many situations, this will be all you need to do. If you need to manipulate the database structure and create and modify tables, columns and indexes within a workflow there are several activities you can use

1. Type Create
2. Type Delete
3. Types Read
4. Type Index Create
5. Type Index Delete
6. Column Create
7. Columns Read by Type

Type Create

Type Create creates a new table or type in the database.

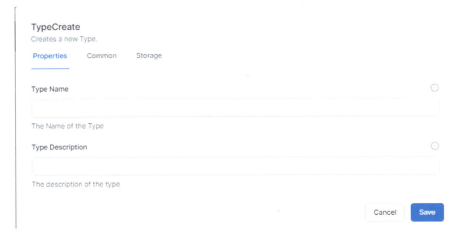

It allows you to enter:

- **Type Name –** the name of the type or table
- **Type Description –** the description of the type

It will create a new type with a single string column called "Title".

It will return the TypeId of the new Type in the activity property of ReturnId.

Type Delete

Type delete will delete a type given its Id.

Types Read

Types Read takes no input parameters and returns a JSON object of all the types in your system

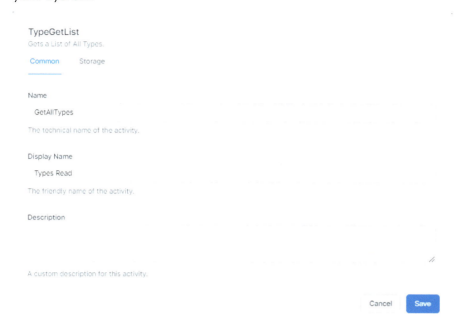

Type Index Create

Indexes are used by databases to lookup information quickly. They keep an index of all the available data in a column and can use it to find information faster than working through each record. Where you will use a column to find data, it is important to establish an index for that column.

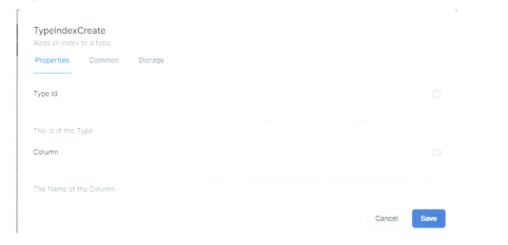

Enter the Type Id and Column Name to create an index for that Column. The activity will return the Id of the column as return Id.

Type Index Delete

Use this activity to delete an index you created previously.

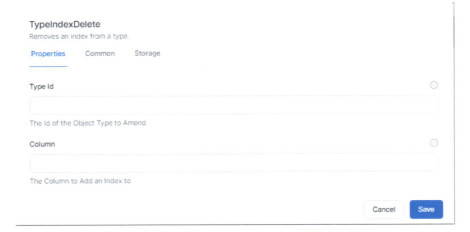

Column Create

Column Create adds a new Column to a Type.

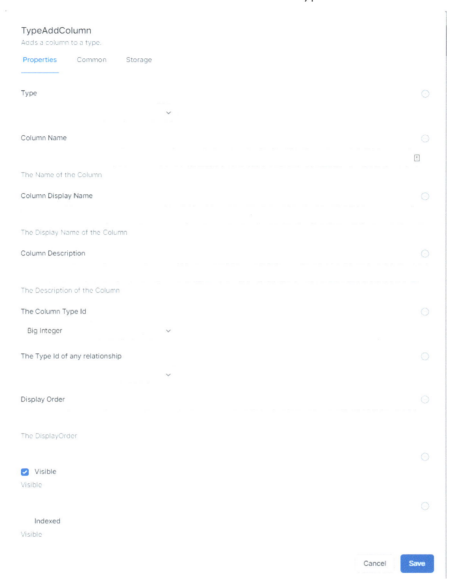

This activity creates a new column for a Type (or Table). Enter the following information:

- **Type** – Choose the type (or table) to add a column for
- **Column Name** – Choose a name for the column. Best practices dictate a single word with no spaces or non text characters.
- **Column Display Name** – Enter the name that will be shown to the end-user in the system for this column.
- **Column Description** – Enter the description of the column so you can understand later what the column is for.
- **Column Type Id** – This is the type of data the column contains. Valid entries are:

- o **Big Integer –** This can be a very large number but is commonly used as a relationship between this and an object in another type. If you wish this to be a relationship, complete the *The Type Id of any relationship* below.
- o **Integer –** This is a whole number, positive or negative, without decimal places.
- o **Decimal 2 –** This is a decimal number with two decimal places, e.g. a currency.
- o **Decimal 5 –** This is a decimal number with five decimal places. It is commonly used for percentages and other numbers that require great precision.
- o **True/False –** This stores the value of true or false
- o **String –** This stores string information, such as text
- o **DateTime –** This is a date/time data stored as UTC and displayed as local time.
- o **Url –** This is a hyperlink or URL.
- o **Embed –** This embeds multimedia such as video
- - **The Type Id of any relationship –** This is the type you want this column to lookup. If so, the **Column Type Id** must be a **Big Integer**
- - **Display Order –** The order this column appears in the User Interface
- - **Visible –** Whether the column is visible to the end user
- - **Indexed –** Whether the column is indexed.

If successful, this activity returns the ColumnId of the newly created column.

Columns Read by Type

This returns all the columns for the selected type. You can choose to return all columns or just visible columns.

The array of columns is returned in the Columns property of this activity.

Data

Once the data structure is in place, you can work with the data itself. The following activities allow you to manipulate data:

- Create Object Instance
- Update Object Instance
- Get Object Instance
- List Object Instances
- List Object Instance History
- JSON Data Insert

Create Object Instance

This activity allows you to create a new object instance and data (sometimes referred to as a row), and to save this new object into a variable.

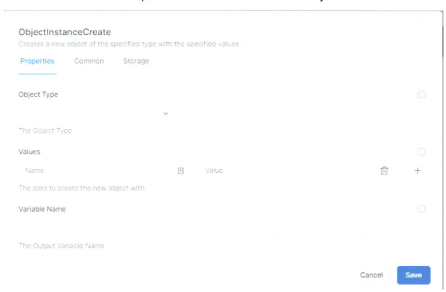

First, select the **Object Type.** Then add any data for the **Columns** for this Type into the **Values** area. Finally enter a **Variable Name** to create a workflow variable containing this new object instance.

This activity also returns **Instance,** which is the new instance created and **InstanceId** which is the Id of the new Instance (or row).

Update Object Instance

This activity allows you to update the data in an instance and optionally clear any fields that are not provided.

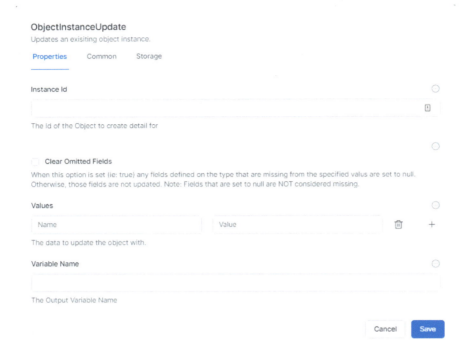

First enterthe **Instance Id of the instance you wantg to update. This might have been returned when you used a** *Create Object Instance* **activity** Next you can choose to **Clear Omitted fields.** That means if this type has a column and you *do **not** include data for it, the data will be cleared.*

You can enter columns and values or present this as JavaScript or a JSON file.

Finally, you can choose a **Variable Name** to have the updated instance (or row) stored in a workflow variable.

The activity will have a property on exit called **Instance** which also contains the updated instance (or row).

Get Object Instance

This activity simply retrieves the current information on an instance (or row) and puts it into a variable.

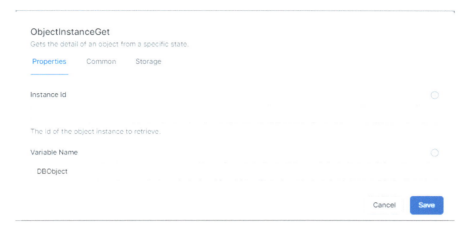

The activity will have a property on exit called **Instance** which also contains the instance (or row).

List Object Instances

This activity retrieves a list of object instances and accepts OData Filters and queries.

See oData Query Syntax for information on constructing OData queries

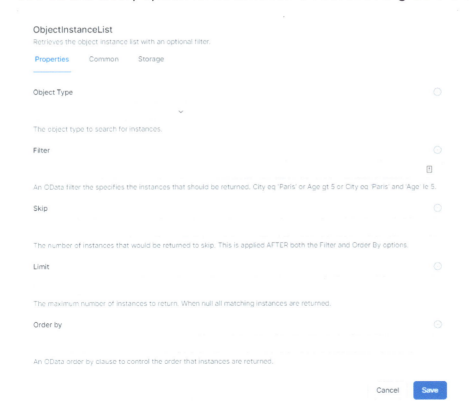

The activity accepts the following inputs:

1. The **Object Type** you wish to get a list for
2. The **Filter** which is an OData filter to filter the records.
3. **Skip-** Once the filter and order by has been performed this selects the record to start from. This is commonly used to retrieve pages of data of a certain size. The value used in *Skip* would normally be a variable that is incremented in a loop.
4. **Limit** – this limits the number of rows to return and is commonly used in conjunction with **Skip** to select a specific page of data.
5. **Order By –** This selects the order in which rows are returned and sorts the data as required.

The activity has a single output property **Output** which includes the requested list. Ensure you give the activity a name under the **Common** tab to ensure you can access this information.

List Object Instance History

Every time you update an instance (or row), the system saves the previous row as history. This can be retrieved using the List Object Instance History activity.

This accepts OData filters and queries.

See oData Query Syntax for information on constructing OData queries

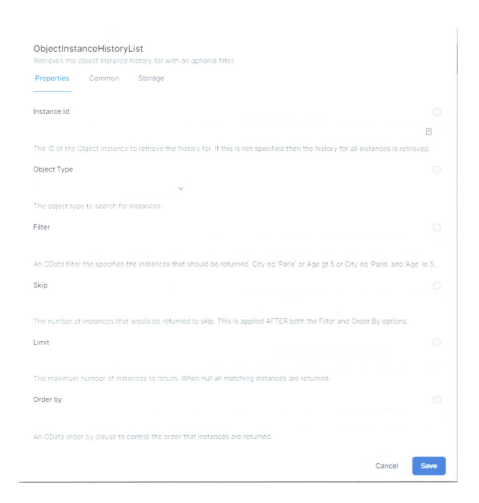

The activity accepts the following inputs:

1. The **Instance Id** for which you wish to get a history list
2. The **Filter** which is an OData filter to filter the records.
3. **Skip-** Once the filter and order by has been performed this selects the record to start from. This is commonly used to retrieve pages of data of a certain size.
4. **Limit** – this limits the number of rows to return and is commonly used in conjunction with **Skip** to select a specific page of data.
5. **Order By –** This selects the order in which rows are returned and sorts the data as required.

The activity has a single output property **Output** which includes the requested list. Ensure you give the activity a name under the **Common** tab to ensure you can access this information.

JSON Data Insert

JSON Data Insert is an activity designed to use JSON data to perform the following:

1. Locate an instance with a matching key field and update the instance (if no match then create a new instance)
2. If a column doesn't exist, create it
3. Add the data to an instance

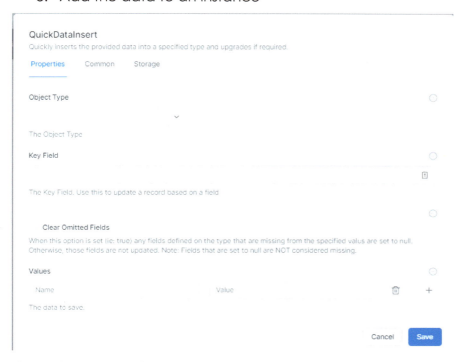

First, select the *Object Type*

Next, select a key field. This is used to identify if this is a new instance or udpate an existing one. If you are using something like JotForm, make this the submission_id.

Finally decide whether to clear omitted fields or not and insert the data, either as JSON or as Name Value entries.

The activity has a single output property **Output** which includes the added or updated instance (or row). Ensure you give the activity a name under the **Common** tab so you can access this information.

Timer Activities

Timer Activities in World of Workflows provide triggers to start and resume workflows based on server time. It should be noted that when working with server time when world of workflows is hosted in Azure, AWS or GCP, the time is always stored in UTC.

This chapter will cover the essential Timer Activities, including CRON, TIMER, START AT AND CLEAR TIMER

CRON

The CRON activity starts a workflow based on a CRON expression. CRON started as a command-line utility, used as a job scheduler on Unix-like operating systems. You can use cron to schedule workflows to run periodically at fixed times, dates, or intervals.

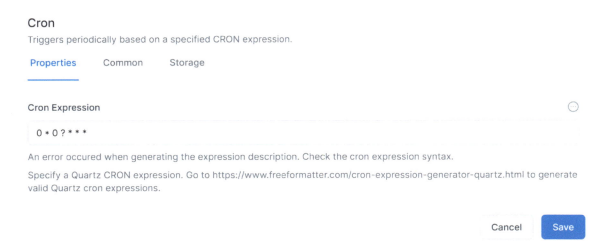

Cron's name originates from chronos, the Greek word for time.

The cron format has five time and date fields separated by at least one blank. There can be no blank within a field value. Scheduled tasks are executed when the minute, hour, and month of year fields match the current time and date, and at least one of the two day fields (day of month, or day of week) match the current date.

Field Name	Allowed Values
Minute	0-59
Hour	0-23
Day of month	1-31
Month	1-12 where 1 is January,2 is February etc Uppercase, lowercase and mixed-case three character strings based on the English name of the month, for example jan, feb, mar, apr etc
Day of week	0-7 where 0 or 7 is Sunday, 1 mis Monday and so on Uppercase, lowercase or mixed case three character strings based on the English name of the day, mon, tue, wed, thu, fri, sat or sun

Ranges and lists

Ranges of numbers are allowed. Ranges are two numbers separated with a hyphen. The specified range is inclusive. For example, the range 8-11 for an hour entry specifies execution at hours 8, 9, 10 and 11.

Lists are allowed. A list is a set of numbers or ranges separated by commas. For example:

1,2,5,9

0-4,8-12

Unrestricted range

A field can contain an asterisk (*), which represents all possible values in the field.

The day of a command's execution can be specified by two fields: day of month and day of week. If both fields are restricted by the use of a value other than the asterisk, the command will run when either field matches the current time. For example, the value 30 4 1,15 * 5 causes a command to run at 4:30 AM on the 1st and 15th of each month, plus every Friday.

Step values

Step values can be used in conjunction with ranges. The syntax range/step defines the range and an execution interval.

If you specify first-last/step, execution takes place at first, then at all successive values that are distant from first by step, until last.

For example, to specify command execution every other hour, use 0-23/2. This expression is equivalent to the value 0,2,4,6,8,10,12,14,16,18,20,22.

If you specify */step, execution takes place at every interval of step through the unrestricted range. For example, as an alternative to 0-23/2 for execution every other hour, use */2.

Example

The following table lists values that you can use CRON activity:

Table 2. Example task schedules and the appropriate schedule argument values

Desired task schedule

Schedule	Value
2:10 PM every Monday	10 14 * * 1
Every day at midnight	0 0 * * *
Every weekday at midnight	0 0 * * 1-5
Midnight on 1st and 15th day of the month	0 0 1,15 * *
6.32 PM on the 17th, 21st and 29th of November plus each Monday and Wednesday in November each year	32 18 17,21,29 11 mon,wed

Timer

The timer activity triggers at a specific timeout. It could run every 10 minutes, every 5 seconds or every hour.

To specify the timeout, you need to use a duration object, expressed as time.

Interval	Meaning
00:00:05	Every 5 seconds
00:02:00	Every 2 minutes
01:00:00	Every hour

Unlike Cron which runs when the system time matches a specific time and date, timer when started runs the duration after the previous run.

StartAt

The StartAt activity triggers at a specific moment in time. If the time is in the past, the activity will not run. If it is in the future, it will wait until the time then start the rest of the workflow.

The date and time should be expressed as UTC and use the following format:

YYYY-MM-DDTHH:mm:ssZ (for example: 2023-07-10T12:00:00Z). This represents a date-time in the UTC timezone.

Clear Timer

ClearTimer, is part of the "Timers" category. Its purpose is to cancel or clear a timer (of types Cron, StartAt, Timer), thus preventing it from executing.

The ClearTimer activity accepts ActivityId. This should be the ID of the timer activity (Cron, StartAt, Timer) that needs to be cleared. This input parameter supports JavaScript and Liquid syntaxes.

To use this, name the activity you want to cancel, then use the JavaScript syntax:

getActivityID("ActivityName")

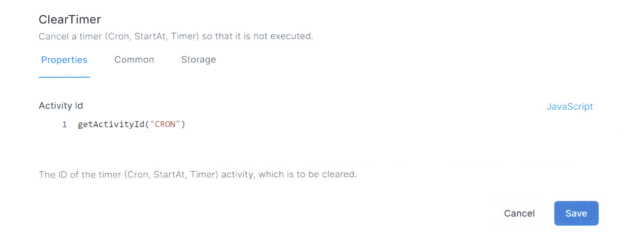

In essence, the ClearTimer activity provides a way to programmatically control the execution of a workflow by allowing timer activities to be cancelled based on certain conditions.

Documentation in World of Workflows

World of Workflows includes comprehensive documentation features that help you maintain an organized and well-documented system. By automatically generating crucial documentation such as data diagrams, data dictionaries, views dictionaries, and detailed workflow information, World of Workflows ensures that your team can easily understand and manage your processes.

This chapter will cover the key aspects of documentation in World of Workflows:

Data (ERD) Diagram

An Entity Relationship Diagram (ERD) is a visual representation of the tables and relationships within your User Configurable Database. World of Workflows automatically generates an ERD for your database, enabling you to quickly grasp the structure and connections between tables. This visualization is invaluable for understanding the overall data architecture and identifying areas for optimization or expansion.

Data Dictionary

The data dictionary is a comprehensive reference of all tables and columns within your User Configurable Database. It includes information such as table and column names, data types, descriptions, and any constraints or relationships. World of Workflows generates a data dictionary to facilitate a clear understanding of the database structure and enable efficient management and development of your data.

Views Dictionary

The views dictionary is a catalog of all the views defined within World of Workflows. It includes information such as view names, descriptions, parent views, and associated fields. The views dictionary aids in managing and understanding the different perspectives and hierarchies of your data, allowing you to create more effective views and improve overall user experience.

Workflow Documentation

World of Workflows provides detailed documentation for each workflow, including:

- Workflow Overview: A summary of the workflow's purpose, description, and key components.

- Activities List: A comprehensive list of all activities used in the workflow, along with their descriptions and configurations.
- Flow Diagram: A visual representation of the workflow's structure, displaying the flow of activities and branching logic. This diagram helps users understand the workflow's design and execution path, making it easier to optimize and maintain.

By offering these robust documentation features, World of Workflows empowers your team to manage and develop your systems effectively. Comprehensive documentation not only promotes a clear understanding of your data and workflows but also helps to ensure that your organization can adapt and scale efficiently as your needs evolve.

Developing Plugins for World of Workflows

World of Workflows features a plugin architecture that enables developers to extend the system's functionality by creating custom Elsa Activities. This chapter will provide an overview of the development process for creating plugins and how to implement custom activities.

Plugin Development Overview

To create a plugin for World of Workflows, you need to develop a C# class library project that includes Elsa and references the HubOneWorkflows.Plugins namespace. This namespace contains the essential interfaces and classes for plugin development, such as ICommand, PluginLoadContext, and PluginOperations.

Creating a Custom Activity

To create a custom Activity, you need to implement a new class that inherits from Elsa.Activity or one of its subclasses. This class should override the required methods to define the activity's behavior, inputs, and outputs.

For example, to create a custom activity that performs a specific calculation, you could implement a class like this:

```csharp
using Elsa;
using Elsa.Attributes;
using Elsa.Expressions;
using Elsa.Results;
using Elsa.Services;
using Elsa.Services.Models;


[ActivityDefinition(Category = "Custom", Description = "Performs a custom calculation")]
public class CustomCalculationActivity : Activity
{
    [ActivityProperty(Hint = "Enter the first number")]
    public double Number1 { get; set; }


    [ActivityProperty(Hint = "Enter the second number")]
    public double Number2 { get; set; }
```

```
    protected override async Task<ActivityExecutionResult>
OnExecuteAsync(WorkflowExecutionContext context, CancellationToken cancellationToken)
    {
        double result = PerformCustomCalculation(Number1, Number2);

        Output.SetVariable("Result", result);

        return Done();
    }


    private double PerformCustomCalculation(double number1, double number2)
    {
        // Perform the custom calculation logic here
    }
}
```

Implementing the ConfigCommand Class

In your plugin project, you need to create a ConfigCommand class that implements the ICommand interface. This class should define the AddActivities method, which adds your custom Elsa Activities to the builder:

```
public class ConfigCommand : ICommand
{
    public Elsa.Options.ElsaOptionsBuilder AddActivities(Elsa.Options.ElsaOptionsBuilder builder)
    {
        builder
            .AddActivity<CreateArmClient>()
            .AddActivity<CreateResourceGroup>();
        return builder;
    }
}
```

Code Signing and Importing the Plugin

Once you've developed your plugin, send the assembly to support@worldofworkflows.com for code signing. After the assembly has been signed, you can import the plugin into World of Workflows:

1. Log in as an administrator.
2. Go to Admin -> Settings -> Developer Mode.
3. Navigate to the Plugins section.
4. Import the signed plugin.

By developing custom plugins for World of Workflows, you can extend the platform's capabilities to better suit your organization's unique requirements. By creating custom Elsa Activities, you can integrate new functionality directly into your workflows, enabling greater flexibility and customization.

Solutions

Solutions are packaged collections of Types, Views and Workflows. Using the Solutions feature of world of workflows, you can export these items and re-import them into another system.

Note: Solutions are compressed into Zip files. Solution Authors can open the zip file and edit the files within prior to sending a solution to someone else.

Exporting Solutions

Navigate to Admin -> Solutions and click the Export button .

Give the solution a name, version, and optional description and icon,

Next, expand **Types, Workflows** and **Views** and select the items you want to include in the solution.

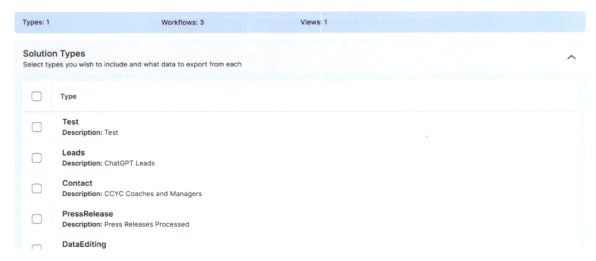

When complete, click **Export Solution.**

The system will download a zip file.

In this zip file are several files:

- **SOLUTION_DETAILS** is a file which contains information on your solution in **JSON** format.

- **SETUP_WF** is a workflow that is run when the solution in imported. It creates all the types, and views. You can modify this workflow to do anything you wish by importing it into World of Workflows, editing it and exporting it.
- **The remaining files** are the workflows you wish to import.

To import a solution

Navigate to Admin -> Solutions and click the green import button [↑].

Click to upload the solution or drag and drop.

Check the Name, Version, Icon and Description are what you expect:

Import a solution

Name

Sln-Export-08-08-2023-3125	Version
	1

Description

| Types: 1 | Workflows: 3 | Views: 1 |

Verify (or deselect) the types, workflows and views.

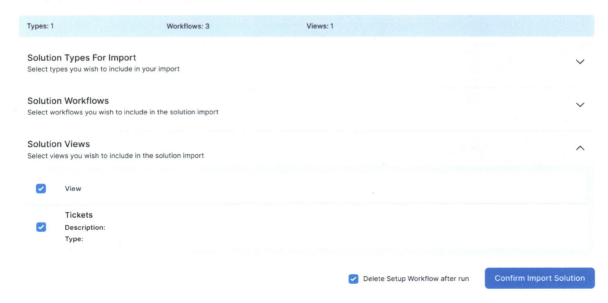

Finally, check whether you want to delete the setup workflow after run and click **Confirm Import Solution.**

Important: Importing solutions is at your own risk. Solutions can contain destructive workflows so ensure you check the solution source and setup workflow before importing.

Examples

This section contains packaged examples of how to solve certain business problems. These are meant to be taken, modified and used by you to solve your own business problems.

Designing long-running workflows

As you develop your workflows, you will have workflows in production which you need to change. It is easy to make these changes and they will apply to all future instances of your workflows. However, if you have a workflow that started before your change was made and has not yet completed, Workd Of Workflows will execute your old workflow.

This diagram describes this scenario:

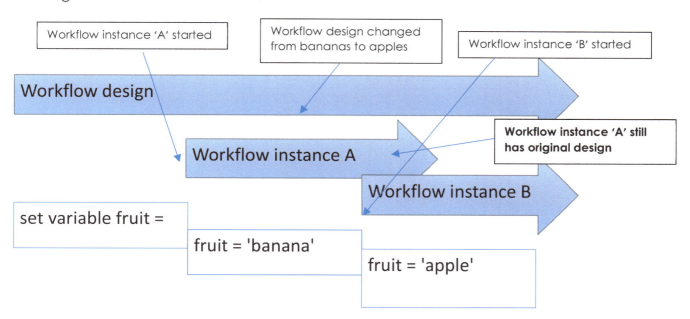

The workflow engine will continue to run your workflows as they were designed until they complete. This maintains the integrity of your design, and you can be confident that the workflow will continue to run the way you design it, even if changes are subsequently made to that workflow.

This can become a problem if you expect your workflows to run for an extended period of time.

For example, your company has a process that manages your employee HR process - from recruitment, onboarding, pay rises and eventual termination of employment.

You could write this as a single workflow, and each time an employee starts with the company a new instance of the workflow would be created. The effect of this is that you would have one instance for Jane Smith's employment, a second instance for John Doe's employment and so forth.

You would expect that your employment process would change during the period of a specific employee's employment. However, the instances that are still running will not inherit any design changes you make to the workflow. We hope and expect that employees will be with us for many years, and change to the workflow during this time is inevitable.

So, how do we manage this?

Firstly, break up your workflows into manageable pieces. Design your workflows so that each one can be completed in a 'reasonable' period of time. This might be a day, a week or month, depending on the workflow and the likelihood of change.

Here is an example of one way to break up this sample workflow.

Each workflow could call the next. For example, changes made to the Pay Rise workflow would now apply to an employee currently being processed by the Onboarding workflow.

What if you have a complex workflow and breaking it into small flows does not suit?

A more challenging example might be a workflow to manage thousands of insurance renewals, where a complex process must run for months and there is a high likelihood of making process improvements whilst thousands of workflow instances are running.

We can imagine breaking your workflows into smaller pieces. Part 2 could be called from Part 1. In Part 2 you may need 20 tasks, some asked in only specific scenarios.

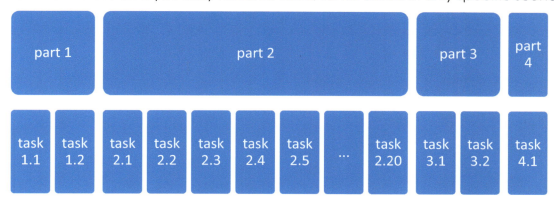

However, changes to Part 2 might need to impact the existing long-running workflow instances. We have developed the Overview workflow concept to manage this.

Implementing an Overview workflow

One way to have a single workflow run for the entire process and still be able to make changes along the way is to use a simple workflow we will call an Overview workflow.

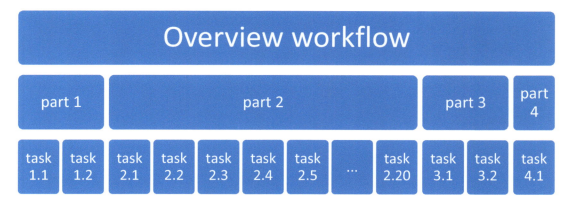

Here is how to design this workflow.

1. Create a workflow, give it a suitable name, such as *HR Overview*.
2. Implement a method to start your *HR Overview* workflow (eg from a data object (see **Implementing triggers**), a timer (see Error! Reference source not found.))
3. Set up any variables you need to pass to the main workflow, such as the ObjectID of the triggering object instance
4. Add a *Run workflow* activity to kick off your main workflow

5. Add a *Run JavaScript* activity to grab the outcome of your main workflow
6. (optional, and recommended for debugging) add a *TaskCreate* activity to provide you with the ability to stop your workflow
7. Join everything up.

You will notice that there is almost nothing in this workflow that will ever need to change. All it does is to call another workflow. The simpler you make your Overview workflow, the less likelihood that it will ever need changes.

Here are the activities in detail

1. The workflow is called *StaffOnboardingOverview*
2. I chose an *Object Instance Trigger* to start this workflow. It is run from within a *Staff* instance:

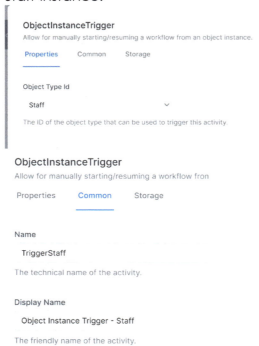

3. Set a variable called **OBJECTID** to contain the ObjectId of the initiating Staff object:

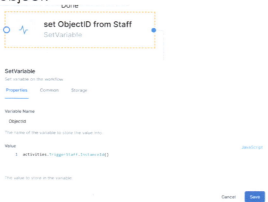

Note: we use JavaScript to get the value, using the **NAME** of the trigger activity to get the ObjectID, using this formula:

`activities.TriggerStaff.InstanceId()`

4. This is the *Run Workflow* activity:

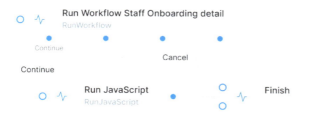

The workflow definition uses a Liquid Filter to allow us to use the name of the workflow we are calling (rather than it's ID)

The Input is the JSON we will be passing to our main workflow

The branches **Continue** & **Cancel** are the text entered into Possible Outcomes.

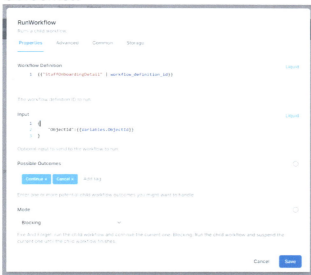

Note the NAME on the next page:

You will use this name in the next activity.

5. The *Run JavaScript* activity

Note how the name of the *Run Workflow* activity is used in the *Run JavaScript*.

```
var parameters =
JSON.parse(activities.runDetailWorkflow.Output().workflowOutput)

for(const property in parameters)
{
    setVariable(property.toString(),parameters[property]);
}
```

6. (Optional) Create a Task to allow you to stop the Overview workflow at will.
   Note the branches

7. Add a Finish activity and connect the activities like this:

Implementing the main workflow

The main workflow can now be designed to be called as many times as needed to ensure that it does not run for too long.

Accept parameters from the Overview workflow

Create this as the first activity in your main workflow:

Use this JavaScript to take the JSON passed from the Overview workflow and convert it to dot-notation variables.

```
var parameters = JSON.parse(input)
setVariable("Parameters",parameters)
```

If the JSON passed in is

```
{
    "ObjectId":123
}
```

This allows you to reference the passed in ObjectId in Liquid as

```
{{Variables.Parameters.ObjectId}}
```

And in JavaScript as

```
getVariable("Parameters").ObjectId
```

Use Status fields as starting points of your main workflow

Use a Switch to direct the flow, using data saved in your object to determine where the flow is up to. For example:

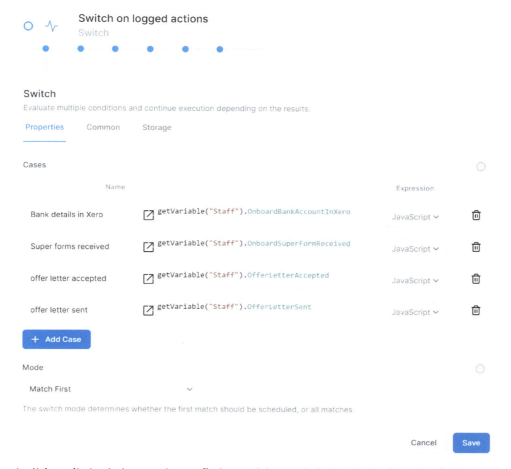

In this switch statement you first want to match the last checkpoint in your workflow then the next-to-last checkpoint, and so on.

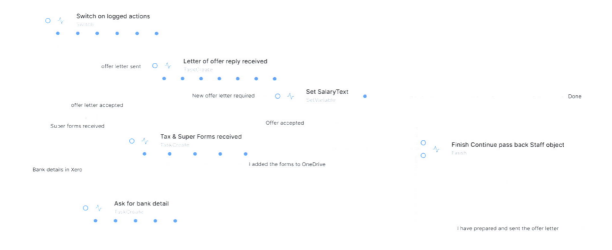

Return to the Overview workflow frequently

This is the Finish activity.

It passes back the ObjectId so that the Overview workflow can use it to call the main workflow again. It also passes back the 'Continue' Outcome, which is used to determine whether to run the main workflow again. (If we pass back 'Cancel', the Overview workflow will stop).

Notice that the main workflow does the minimum amount of processing between the switch statement and the finish statement, ideally just enough to prepare and process one *Task Create* activity. This is where the magic occurs: now the main workflow only has to be in existence for one task at a time. As soon as this task is complete, a new instance of the main workflow is created, and continued from this checkpoint.

Ensure variables are available

Note that you will need to ensure the variables you set in your main workflow are available when the workflow is restarted. This can be done by calling a 'set variables' workflow, or specifically in the main workflow.

Example of a 'set variables' workflow:

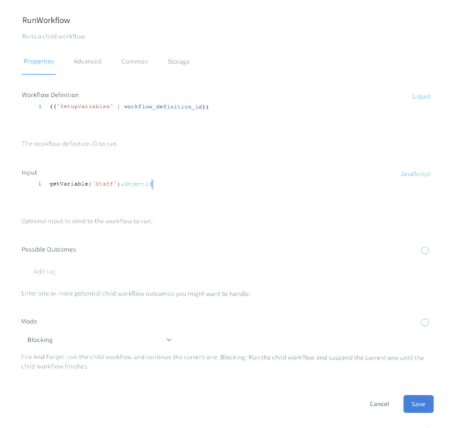

We pass in a suitable ObjectID that we are always going to know.

Note that *Mode* is **BLOCKING**, waiting for the *SetupVariables* workflow to complete.

The first activity in the *SetupVariables* workflow is to get the database object using the passed in ObjectId. For example:

The rest of the variables are then set up

The last 2 activities in the SetupVariables workflow are to set up send back the variables to the calling workflow

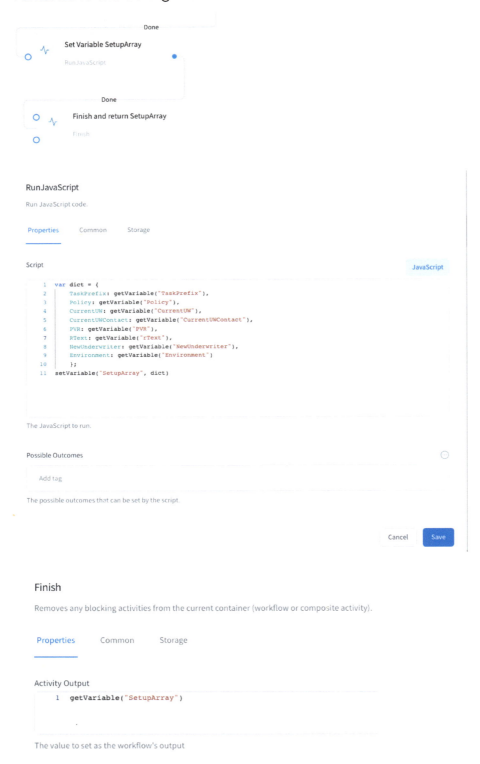

RunJavaScript

Run JavaScript code.

Properties Common Storage

Script   JavaScript

```
1   var dict = {
2       TaskPrefix: getVariable("TaskPrefix"),
3       Policy: getVariable("Policy"),
4       CurrentUW: getVariable("CurrentUW"),
5       CurrentUWContact: getVariable("CurrentUWContact"),
6       PVR: getVariable("PVR"),
7       RText: getVariable("rText"),
8       NewUnderwriter: getVariable("NewUnderwriter"),
9       Environment: getVariable("Environment")
10      };
11  setVariable("SetupArray", dict)
```

The JavaScript to run.

Possible Outcomes

Add tag

The possible outcomes that can be set by the script.

Cancel   Save

Finish

Removes any blocking activities from the current container (workflow or composite activity).

Properties Common Storage

Activity Output

```
1   getVariable("SetupArray")
```

The value to set as the workflow's output

Another method of setting variables in the main workflow is to build up the variables from the known data. For example, in this case, if the Staff already has a SalaryPackage we can get the SalaryPackage object from the Staff object. Otherwise we can create the SalaryPackage object and save the relationship back to the Staff object

Reference

This section contains reference information on the platform.

Data Types

Data types is the name given to field types in the database. By using data types, you can control how data is stored in the database and how it is displayed to the end user. The following datatypes are available in World of Workflows:

ID	DATA TYPE	USE
1	Big Integer	The Big Integer data type is commonly used to reference another Type, but can be used anywhere an extremely large whole number is required.
2	Integer	The Integer data type is used where a whole positive or negative number is required.
3	Decimal 2	This is a decimal number with two digits of precision, commonly used for representing monetary amounts.
4	Decimal 5	This is a decimal number with 5 digits of precision, commonly used for representing floating point numbers.
5	True/False	This is commonly known as the Boolean data type and holds anything that can have only two values.
6	String	Strings are any length collections of character strings, stored in UTF-8
7	DateTime	Stored in the database as UTC DateTime and shown in the interface as local datetime, The DateTime DataType is used for storing dates and times or both.
8	Url	This is a string which represents a hyperlink
9	Embed	This is a string which can contain a html embed code.

Note on storing Binary in the database. We have deliberately chosen not to provide a binary data type, Instead we recommend to use JavaScript inside of workflows to Base64Encode/Decode and store the data in a String DataType. This is because of direct limitations of some of our supported database platforms not allowing binary types.

Activity List

The following section is a comprehensive list of activities available in the platform, noting that you can extend the platform using plugins.

Compensation

Compensable activities in Elsa Workflows refer to actions that can be compensated or "undone" if certain conditions are not met or if an error occurs during the execution of a workflow. Compensable activities are essential for ensuring the integrity and reliability of the workflow processes, particularly in scenarios where multiple steps are involved, and the correct execution of each step is crucial for the overall success of the process.

Compensable activities have the following characteristics:

- **Reversibility**: A compensable activity has a corresponding "undo" operation that can be executed to reverse its effects and return the system to its previous state before the activity was executed. This is useful for handling errors and maintaining data consistency.
- **Idempotency**: Compensable activities are designed to be idempotent, meaning they can be executed multiple times without causing any side effects or changing the outcome. This ensures that compensating actions will not introduce new errors or inconsistencies in the system.
- **Transactional nature**: Compensable activities are often used in conjunction with transactions to ensure that a series of related actions are either all completed successfully or none of them are. If any activity in the transaction fails, the compensating actions are executed to reverse the completed activities, maintaining the system's consistency
- **Error handling**: Compensable activities allow for robust error handling, as they can be used to automatically roll back a workflow to a previous state if an error occurs. This helps to minimize the risk of data corruption or other issues that may arise from failed operations.

In Workflows, compensable activities would be designed and implemented as part of the overall workflow, with each activity having a clearly defined compensating action. This ensures that any errors or inconsistencies can be effectively addressed, maintaining the system's stability and reliability.

The following are the activities available for compensation:

Compensable

Allows work that is executed after this activity to be undone.

Compensate

Invokes a specific compensable activity.

Confirm

Confirms a specific compensable activity.

Console Activities

In Elsa Workflows, Console Activities are used for simple input and output operations to interact with the user through the console. They are helpful for gathering data, providing status updates, or displaying results. There are two main Console Activities in Elsa Workflows: Read Line and Write Line.

Read Line

The Read Line Activity is used to read a line of text input from the user through the console. This activity allows you to gather data or responses from the user during the execution of a workflow.

1. Add the Read Line Activity to your workflow where you want to capture user input.
2. Optionally, you can provide a custom prompt by setting the 'Prompt' property. This text will be displayed to the user before they enter their input.
3. After the activity is executed, the user's input will be stored in the specified output variable (e.g., 'UserInput').

You can then use the captured input in subsequent activities or for decision-making within the workflow.

Note: Although Read Line is available, it will not work as World of Workflows runs as a service and cannot interact with the console.

Write Line

The Write Line Activity is used to display a line of text to the user through the console. This activity is useful for providing status updates, displaying results, or giving instructions to the user during the workflow execution.

1. Add the Write Line Activity to your workflow where you want to display text to the user.
2. Set the 'Text' property to the message you want to display. You can use static text or include variables and expressions to display dynamic content.
3. When the activity is executed, the specified text will be displayed on the console.

You can use the Write Line Activity multiple times throughout your workflow to provide updates or information to the user as needed.

By incorporating these Console Activities into your Elsa Workflows, you can create more interactive and user-friendly processes that allow for better communication between the system and the end user.

Note: Although Write Line is available, it will not usefully work as World of Workflows runs as a service and cannot interact with the console.

Control Flow

In Elsa Workflows, control flow activities are used to manage the execution order of activities within a workflow and to implement conditional logic or looping constructs. They help to create dynamic and flexible processes based on the specific requirements of your use case. Some common control flow activities in Elsa Workflows include:

If-Else

The *If-Else* Activity allows you to define conditional branches in your workflow, executing different sets of activities based on a specified condition.

1. Add the *If-Else* Activity to your workflow where you want to introduce conditional logic.
2. Set the CONDITION property to an expression that evaluates to either true or false.
3. Connect the TRUE outcome to the activities that should be executed if the condition is true.
4. Connect the FALSE outcome to the activities that should be executed if the condition is false.

While

The *While* Activity is used to create loops in your workflow, repeatedly executing a set of activities as long as a specified condition is true.

1. Add the *While* Activity to your workflow where you want to create a loop.
2. Set the CONDITION property to an expression that evaluates to either true or false.
   a. Connect the LOOP outcome to the activities that should be executed within the loop. Use the CURRENTITEM property within the iteration activities to access the current item in the collection.
   b. Note that these activities may be executed many times. The last of these activities will normally have no outcome.
3. Connect the DONE outcome to the activities that should be executed after the loop has finished.

ForEach

The *ForEach* Activity iterates over a collection of items, executing a set of activities for each item in the collection.

1. Add the *ForEach* Activity to your workflow where you want to iterate over a collection.
2. Set the **COLLECTION** property to a collection or an expression that evaluates to a collection.
3. Connect the **ITERATION** outcome to the activities that should be executed for each item in the collection.
   a. Use the **CURRENTITEM** property within the iteration activities to access the current item in the collection.
   b. Note that these activities may be executed many times. The last of these activities will normally have no outcome.
4. Connect the **DONE** outcome to the activities that should be executed after the iteration has completed.

Switch

The *Switch* Activity is used to create multiple branches in your workflow based on the value of a specified expression.

1. Add the *Switch* Activity to your workflow where you want to create multiple branches.
2. Set the **EXPRESSION** property to an expression that evaluates to a value used for branching.
3. Add one or more **CASE** outcomes, each with a value that corresponds to a possible result of the *expression*.
4. Connect each **CASE** outcome to the activities that should be executed for that specific value.
5. Optionally, you can add a **DEFAULT** outcome, which will be executed if none of the case values match the expression result.

Break

The *Break* Activity in Elsa Workflows is a control flow activity used to exit a loop prematurely. It allows you to terminate the execution of activities within a loop when a specified condition is met, instead of waiting for the loop's original exit condition. The Break Activity is particularly useful when working with While and ForEach activities, providing a way to break out of the loop based on custom criteria.

1. Add the *Break* Activity to your workflow within a loop (created using a *While* or *ForEach* activity).
2. Set a condition or trigger for the *Break* Activity. This can be done using an If-Else Activity, or by incorporating a condition directly into the Break Activity.
3. When the *Break* Activity is executed, the workflow will exit the current loop immediately, skipping the remaining activities in the loop and moving on to the next activity connected to the loop's **DONE** outcome.

For example, if you are using a *While* Activity to process a list of items and you want to stop processing when a specific item is encountered, you could use an *If-Else* Activity within the loop to check for that item. If the item is found, the *If-Else* Activity would execute the *Break* Activity, immediately stopping the loop and moving on to the next activity outside the loop.

The *Break* Activity helps to improve the efficiency and flexibility of workflows, allowing you to create more dynamic and responsive processes that can adapt to different conditions during runtime.

For

The *For* Activity is a control flow activity in Elsa Workflows that allows you to create loops with a predefined number of iterations. This activity is useful for executing a set of activities a specific number of times, providing a more controlled and predictable looping construct compared to the While Activity.

1. Add the *For* Activity to your workflow where you want to create a loop with a fixed number of iterations.
2. Set the START property to the initial value of the loop counter (usually 0 or 1, depending on your requirements).
3. Set the END property to the value at which the loop counter should stop (exclusive). The loop will iterate as long as the loop counter is less than the END'value.
4. Optionally, set the STEP property to define the increment value for each iteration. By default, the 'Step' value is typically 1, meaning the loop counter will increment by 1 after each iteration.
5. Connect the ITERATION outcome to the activities that should be executed within the loop.
6. Connect the DONE outcome to the activities that should be executed after the loop has finished.

Use the CURRENTINDEX property within the loop activities to access the current value of the loop counter.

Here's an example of how the *For* Activity might be used in a workflow:

- Start value: 0
- End value: 5
- Step value: 1

In this example, the loop would execute the activities connected to the ITERATION outcome five times (with loop counter values of 0, 1, 2, 3, and 4). Once the loop counter reaches 5, the loop will exit, and the activities connected to the DONE outcome will be executed.

The *For* Activity provides a structured and straightforward way to create loops in Elsa Workflows, enabling you to implement repetitive tasks with a predictable number of iterations.

Fork

The *Fork* Activity in Elsa Workflows is a control flow activity that allows you to create parallel branches of execution within your workflow. It enables you to split the workflow into multiple paths that can be executed concurrently, improving the efficiency and performance of your processes by allowing tasks to be completed simultaneously.

1. Add the *Fork* Activity to your workflow where you want to create parallel branches of execution.
2. Create the **BRANCHES** by using meaningful names, so that your workflow is easy to read
3. Connect the *Fork* Activity to multiple subsequent activities, *each* representing a separate branch of execution. Each connection from the Fork Activity represents a new parallel path.
4. We do not require a Join activity to wait for all branches in World of Workflows. The Join Activity would usually wait for all the parallel branches to complete before continuing with the subsequent activities in the workflow.

For example, imagine you have a workflow where you need to perform three separate tasks (Task A, Task B, and Task C) that can be executed independently and concurrently. You could use the Fork Activity to create three parallel branches, one for each task, improving the overall performance of the workflow by completing the tasks simultaneously.

Here's a simplified representation of the workflow:

```
              [Fork]
        /       |       \
[Task A]  [Task B]  [Task C]
        \       |       /
              [Join]
```

The Fork Activity is a powerful tool for optimizing your workflows, allowing you to take advantage of parallel processing and improving the overall performance and efficiency of your processes.

Join

The *Join* Activity in Elsa Workflows is a control flow activity used to synchronize multiple parallel branches of execution back into a single path. It is typically used in conjunction with the Fork Activity, which creates parallel branches in the workflow for concurrent execution. The Join Activity ensures that all parallel branches have completed before the workflow proceeds to the next activity in the sequence.

1. After using a *Fork* Activity to create parallel branches of execution, add the *Join* Activity at the point where you want to merge the parallel branches back into a single path.

2. Connect each parallel branch to the *Join* Activity.
3. When the *Join* Activity is reached during workflow execution, it will wait until all connected parallel branches have completed their execution.
4. Once all parallel branches have finished, the Join Activity will allow the workflow to continue with the subsequent activities connected to it.

For example, imagine you have a workflow with three parallel tasks (Task A, Task B, and Task C) created using the Fork Activity. The Join Activity would be used to ensure that all three tasks have completed before the workflow proceeds to the next step, such as processing the combined results of the tasks.

Here's a simplified representation of the workflow:

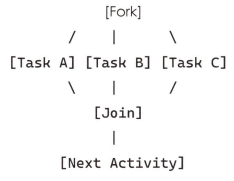

```
            [Fork]
        /     |       \
[Task A] [Task B] [Task C]
        \     |      /
            [Join]
               |
        [Next Activity]
```

Note: there is also the option of allowing the *Join* activity to continue when any one of the connected branches reaches the *Join* Activity.

The *Join* Activity is essential for managing parallel branches in Elsa Workflows, ensuring that all concurrent tasks are completed before the workflow moves on to subsequent activities. This enables you to maintain control and consistency in your processes, while still benefiting from the performance improvements provided by parallel execution.

Parallel for Each

The *Parallel ForEach* Activity in Elsa Workflows is a control flow activity that enables concurrent execution of a set of activities for each item in a collection. It is similar to the standard *ForEach* Activity, but with the added benefit of parallel processing to improve performance and efficiency. The Parallel ForEach Activity is particularly useful when working with large collections or when executing time-consuming tasks that can be processed independently.

1. Add the *Parallel ForEach* Activity to your workflow where you want to concurrently iterate over a collection of items.
2. Set the 'Collection' property to the collection you want to iterate over or an expression that evaluates to a collection.
3. Connect the 'Iteration' outcome to the activities that should be executed for each item in the collection. These activities will be executed in parallel for each item, potentially improving the overall performance of the workflow.
4. Connect the 'Done' outcome to the activities that should be executed after the parallel iteration has completed.

5. Use the 'CurrentItem' property within the iteration activities to access the current item in the collection.

It's important to note that when using the Parallel ForEach Activity, you need to ensure that the activities within the loop can be executed concurrently without causing issues such as data corruption or race conditions. This may require additional synchronization mechanisms, such as locks or semaphores, depending on the specific activities being executed.

The Parallel ForEach Activity provides a powerful and efficient way to process collections in Elsa Workflows, enabling you to take advantage of parallel processing to improve the performance of your processes.

Switch

The Switch Activity in Elsa Workflows is a control flow activity that allows you to create multiple branches of execution based on the value of a specified expression. It enables you to route the workflow to different sets of activities depending on the evaluated result, making your workflow more dynamic and adaptable to various situations.

1. Add the *Switch* Activity to your workflow where you want to create multiple branches based on a specific value or condition.
2. Set the **EXPRESSION** property to an expression that evaluates to a value used for branching. This value will determine which branch of execution the workflow will follow.
3. Add one or more **CASE** outcomes, each with a value that corresponds to a possible result of the expression. The value of the **CASE** outcome should match the expected result of the expression to create a connection to the corresponding branch of activities.
4. Connect each **CASE** outcome to the activities that should be executed for that specific value. These activities represent the different branches that the workflow can take based on the evaluation of the expression.
5. Optionally, you can add a **DEFAULT** outcome, which will be executed if none of the case values match the expression result. This outcome acts as a catch-all for any unexpected or unhandled values.

Here's an example of how the *Switch* Activity might be used in a workflow:

- Expression: OrderStatus

Assuming that OrderStatus is a *variable* that can have the values **NEW**, **PROCESSING**, or **COMPLETE**, you would create three **CASE** outcomes with these values, and connect each outcome to the respective activities that should be executed for each status:

```
      [Switch]
     /    |    \
  New  Proc.  Complete
  /      |       \
[...] [....] [.....]
```

The *Switch* Activity allows you to create more dynamic and flexible workflows that can adapt to different situations based on the evaluation of specific conditions or values. This enables you to build more efficient and responsive processes tailored to the specific needs of your use case.

Email Activities

Email activities are designed to work with SMTP Email Systems. For Office 365, please see the *Send Http* activity and communicate with Microsoft graph as shown in the examples.

Send Email

The *SendEmail* Activity in Elsa Workflows is an action activity that allows you to send an email as part of your workflow. This activity can be used to notify users or stakeholders, send reports, or provide status updates based on the events and outcomes of your workflow. The *SendEmail* Activity typically requires integration with an email service or SMTP server to handle the actual sending of the email.

1. Add the *SendEmail* Activity to your workflow where you want to send an email.
2. Configure the email service or SMTP server settings, if required. This step depends on the specific implementation of Elsa Workflows and might involve setting up API keys, credentials, or other configuration options to connect with the email service. This configuration should be set in the appsettings.json file in the installation folder of World of Workflows.
3. Set the **FROM** property to the email address you want the email to be sent from. This is typically your own email address or an address associated with your application or organization.
4. Set the **TO** property to the recipient's email address or a list of email addresses if you want to send the email to multiple recipients.
5. Set the **SUBJECT** property to the subject line of the email.
6. Set the **BODY** property to the content of the email. This can be plain text or HTML, depending on the capabilities of the SendEmail Activity implementation and the email service being used.
7. Optionally, you can configure additional properties such as **CC**, **BCC**, **REPLYTO**, or **ATTACHMENTS**, depending on the specific implementation of the *SendEmail* Activity and your requirements.

8. Connect the *SendEmail* Activity to other activities in your workflow as needed. You might want to use control flow activities like *If-Else* or *Switch* to determine when the email should be sent or what content it should contain.

The *SendEmail* Activity enables you to integrate email notifications and communication directly into your Elsa Workflows, allowing you to automate notifications, alerts, and updates as part of your overall process automation.

File Activities

File Activities in Elsa Workflows refer to a set of activities that allow you to interact with the file system to perform various operations, such as reading, writing, creating, or deleting files and directories. These activities enable you to incorporate file management tasks into your workflows and automate processes that involve file manipulation.

Some common File Activities in Elsa Workflows include:

Read File

The *ReadFile* Activity is used to read the contents of a file and store the data in a variable or output property for further processing in the workflow.

1. Add the *ReadFile* Activity to your workflow where you want to read a file.
2. Set the **FILEPATH** property to the path of the file you want to read.
3. Connect the *ReadFile* Activity to other activities that will process the file's content or use it as input.

WriteFile

The *WriteFile* Activity allows you to write data to a file, either creating a new file or overwriting an existing one.

1. Add the *WriteFile* Activity to your workflow where you want to write data to a file.
2. Set the **FILEPATH** property to the path of the file you want to write.
3. Set the **CONTENT** property to the data you want to write to the file.
4. Configure the **APPEND** property if you want to append data to the existing file instead of overwriting it.

DeleteFile

The *DeleteFile* Activity is used to delete a file from the file system.

1. Add the *DeleteFile* Activity to your workflow where you want to delete a file.

---

2. Set the **FILEPATH** property to the path of the file you want to delete.
3. Connect the DeleteFile Activity to other activities that may depend on the deletion of the file.

These *File* Activities allow you to integrate file management tasks into your Elsa Workflows, helping you automate processes that involve file manipulation and improving the overall efficiency of your workflows.

By using these control flow activities, you can create complex and dynamic workflows that adapt to varying situations and requirements, enabling more efficient and flexible process automation.

oData Query Syntax

Introduction

The Open Data Protocol (oData) is an open standard that defines a set of best practices for building and consuming RESTful APIs. oData enables the creation of HTTP-based data services, allowing clients to interact with data sources in a standardized and platform-agnostic way. This document provides a comprehensive guide to oData query syntax, which allows clients to filter, sort, and manipulate data retrieved from oData services.

System Query Options

System query options are used to specify the data requested from an oData service. These options can be combined to create complex queries. The following system query options are available:

$filter

The *$filter* option is used to filter the data returned by an oData service based on specified criteria. It supports a range of logical, arithmetic, and comparison operators.

```
/EntitySet?$filter=filter_expression
```

Examples:

- Filter products with a PRICE greater than 20:
  ```
  /Products?$filter=Price gt 20
  ```
- Filter orders with a STATUS of 'Shipped':
  ```
  /Orders?$filter=Status eq 'Shipped'
  ```

$select

The *$select* option is used to specify a subset of properties to return for each entity in the result set. This can reduce the amount of data transmitted over the network.

```
/EntitySet?$select=property1,property2
```

Examples:

- Select only the **NAME** and **PRICE** properties for products:
    ```
    /Products?$select=Name,Price
    ```
- Select only the **ORDERID** and **CUSTOMERNAME** for orders:
    ```
    /Orders?$select=OrderID,CustomerName
    ```

$orderby

The *$orderby* option is used to sort the results of a query by one or more properties in ascending or descending order.

```
/EntitySet?$orderby=property1 asc/desc,property2 asc/desc
```

Examples:

- Order products by **PRICE** in ascending order:
    ```
    /Products?$orderby=Price asc
    ```
- Order orders by **ORDERDATE** in descending order:
    ```
    /Orders?$orderby=OrderDate desc
    ```

$top

The $top option is used to limit the number of results returned by a query.

```
/EntitySet?$top=number
```

Examples:

- Retrieve the **TOP 5** products:
    ```
    /Products?$top=5
    ```
- Retrieve the **TOP 10** orders:
    ```
    /Orders?$top=10
    ```

$skip

The $skip option is used to skip a specified number of results before returning the remaining results.

```
/EntitySet?$skip=number
```

Examples:

- Skip the first 5 products:
  ```
  /Products?$skip=5
  ```
- Skip the first 10 orders:
  ```
  /Orders?$skip=10
  ```

$count

The $count option is used to return the number of entities in the result set.

```
/EntitySet?$count=true
```

Examples:

- Count the number of Products:
  ```
  /Products?$count=true
  ```
- Count the number of Orders:
  ```
  /Orders?$count=true
  ```

Query Functions

oData also provides a set of functions to perform operations on the data. These functions can be used within $filter and $orderby expressions.

String Functions

- *substringof*: Checks if a substring is within a string.
- *length*: Returns the length of a string.

- *indexof*: Returns the starting position of a substring in a string.
- *substring*: Returns a substring from a string.
- *tolower*: Converts a string to lowercase.
- *toupper*: Converts a string to uppercase.
- *trim*: Removes leading and trailing whitespace from a string.
- *concat*: Concatenates two strings.

Date Functions

- *year*: Returns the year component of a date.
- *month*: Returns the month component of a date.
- *day*: Returns the day component of a date.
- *hour*: Returns the hour component of a date.
- *minute*: Returns the minute component of a date.
- *second*: Returns the second component of a date.

Math Functions

- *round*: Rounds a number to the nearest integer.
- *floor*: Rounds a number down to the nearest integer.
- *ceiling*: Rounds a number up to the nearest integer.

Querying Related Entities

oData enables querying related entities using navigation properties. Navigation properties are used to represent relationships between entities.

Expanding Related Entities

The $expand option is used to include related entities in the result set.

```
/EntitySet?$expand=NavigationProperty
```

Examples:

- Retrieve orders along with their ORDERDETAILS:

```
/Orders?$expand=OrderDetails
```

- Retrieve products along with their SUPPLIER information:

```
/Products?$expand=Supplier
```

Filtering Related Entities

You can also apply filters to related entities using the $filter option.

```
Syntax:
/EntitySet?$expand=NavigationProperty($filter=filter_expression)
```

Examples:

- Retrieve *Orders* along with their shipped *OrderDetails*:

```
/Orders?$expand=OrderDetails($filter=Status eq 'Shipped')
```

- Retrieve *Products* along with their active *Supplier* information:

```
/Products?$expand=Supplier($filter=IsActive eq true)
```

Combining Query Options

You can combine multiple query options to create complex queries.

Examples:

- Retrieve the top 10 products with a price greater than 20, ordered by price in ascending order, and select only the Name and Price properties:

```
/Products?$filter=Price gt 20&$orderby=Price
asc&$top=10&$select=Name,Price
```

- Retrieve orders with a status of 'Shipped', skip the first 5 orders, and expand the related customer information:

```
/Orders?$filter=Status eq 'Shipped'&$skip=5&$expand=Customer
```

Liquid in World of Workflows

Liquid is an open-source template language created by Shopify and written in Ruby. It is the backbone of Shopify themes and is used to load dynamic content on storefronts.

Liquid has been in production use at Shopify since 2006 and is now used by many other hosted web applications.

The following sections contain information about the Liquid template language.

Introduction

Liquid uses a combination of objects, tags, and filters inside template files to display dynamic content.

Objects

Objects contain the content that Liquid displays on a page. Objects and variables are displayed when enclosed in double curly braces: {{ and }}.

Input

```
{{ page.title }}
```

Output

```
In this case, Liquid is rendering the content of the title property
of the page object, which contains the text Introduction.
```

Tags

Tags create the logic and control flow for templates. The curly brace percentage delimiters ```{%``` and ```%}``` and the text that they surround do not produce any visible output when the template is rendered. This lets you assign variables and create conditions or loops without showing any of the Liquid logic on the page.

Input

```
{% if user %}
  Hello {{ user.name }}!
```

```
{% endif %}
```

Output

```
Hello Adam!
```

Tags can be categorized into various types:

- Control flow
- Iteration
- Template
- Variable assignment

You can read more about each type of tag in their respective sections.

Filters

Filters change the output of a Liquid object or variable. They are used within double curly braces {{ }} and variable assignment, and are separated by a pipe character |.

Input

```
{{ "/my/fancy/url" | append: ".html" }}
```

Output

Multiple filters can be used on one output, and are applied from left to right.

Input

```
{{ "adam!" | capitalize | prepend: "Hello " }}
```

Output

```
Hello Adam!
```

Operators

Liquid includes many logical and comparison operators. You can use operators to create logic with control flow tags.

Basic operators

Operator	Description
==	equals
!=	does not equal
>	greater than
<	less than
>=	greater than or equal to
<=	less than or equal to
or	logical or
and	logical and

For example:

```
{% if product.title == "Awesome Shoes" %}
  These shoes are awesome!
{% endif %}
```

You can do multiple comparisons in a tag using the *and* & *or* operators:

```
{% if product.type == "Shirt" or product.type == "Shoes" %}
  This is a shirt or a pair of shoes.
{% endif %}
```

contains

contains checks for the presence of a substring inside a string.

```
{% if product.title contains "Pack" %}
  This product's title contains the word Pack.
{% endif %}
```

contains can also check for the presence of a string in an array of strings.

```
{% if product.tags contains "Hello" %}
  This product has been tagged with "Hello".
{% endif %}
```

contains can only search strings. You cannot use it to check for an object in an array of objects.

Order of operations

In tags with more than one *and* or *or* operator, operators are checked in order from right to left. You cannot change the order of operations using parentheses — parentheses are invalid characters in Liquid and will prevent your tags from working.

```
{% if true or false and false %}
  This evaluates to true, since the `and` condition is checked
first.
{% endif %}
{% if true and false and false or true %}
  This evaluates to false, since the tags are checked like this:

  true and (false and (false or true))
  true and (false and true)
  true and false
  false
{% endif %}
```

Truthy and falsy

When a non-boolean data type is used in a boolean context (such as a conditional tag), Liquid decides whether to evaluate it as true or false. Data types that return true by default are called truthy. Data types that return false by default are called falsy.

Truthy

All values in Liquid are truthy except nil and false.

In the example below, the text "Tobi" is not a boolean, but it is truthy in a conditional:

```
{% assign name = "Tobi" %}

{% if name %}
  This text will always appear since "name" is defined.
{% endif %}
```

Strings, even when empty, are truthy. The example below will create empty HTML tags if page.category exists but is empty:

Input

```
{% if page.category %}
  <h1>{{ page.category }}</h1>
{% endif %}
```

Output

```
<h1></h1>
```

Falsy

The only values that are falsy in Liquid are nil and false.

Summary

The table below summarizes what is truthy or falsy in Liquid.

	truthy	falsy
true	•	
false		•
nil		•
string	•	
empty string	•	
0	•	
integer	•	
float	•	
array	•	
empty array	•	
page	•	
EmptyDrop	•	

Types

Liquid objects can be one of six types:

- String
- Number
- Boolean
- Nil
- Array
- EmptyDrop

You can initialize Liquid variables using assign or capture tags.

String

Strings are sequences of characters wrapped in single or double quotes:

```
{% assign my_string = "Hello World!" %}
```
Liquid does not convert escape sequences into special characters.

Number

Numbers include floats and integers:

```
{% assign my_int = 25 %}
{% assign my_float = -39.756 %}
```

Boolean

Booleans are either true or false. No quotations are necessary when declaring a boolean:

```
{% assign foo = true %}
{% assign bar = false %}
```

Nil

Nil is a special empty value that is returned when Liquid code has no results. It is **not** a string with the characters "nil".

Nil is treated as false in the conditions of *if* blocks and other Liquid tags that check the truthfulness of a statement.

In the following example, if the user does not exist (that is, user returns nil), Liquid will not print the greeting:

```
{% if user %}
   Hello {{ user.name }}!
{% endif %}
```

Tags or outputs that return *nil* will not print anything to the page.

Input

```
The current user is {{ user.name }}
```

Output

```
The current user is
```

Array

Arrays hold lists of variables of any type.

Accessing items in arrays

To access all the items in an array, you can loop through each item in the array using an iteration tag.

Input

```
<!-- if site.users = "Tobi", "Laura", "Tetsuro", "Adam" -->
{% for user in site.users %}
  {{ user }}
{% endfor %}
```

Output

```
Tobi Laura Tetsuro Adam
```

Accessing specific items in arrays

You can use square bracket [ ] notation to access a specific item in an array. Array indexing starts at zero. A negative index will count from the end of the array.

Input

```
<!-- if site.users = "Tobi", "Laura", "Tetsuro", "Adam" -->
{{ site.users[0] }}
{{ site.users[1] }}
{{ site.users[-1] }}
```

Output

```
Tobi
Laura
Adam
```

Initializing arrays

You cannot initialize arrays using only Liquid.

You can, however, use the split filter to break a string into an array of substrings.

EmptyDrop

An EmptyDrop object is returned if you try to access a deleted object. In the example below, page_1, page_2 and page_3 are all EmptyDrop objects:

```
{% assign variable = "hello" %}
{% assign page_1 = pages[variable] %}
{% assign page_2 = pages["does-not-exist"] %}
{% assign page_3 = pages.this-handle-does-not-exist %}
```

Checking for emptiness

You can check to see if an object exists or not before you access any of its attributes.

```
{% unless pages == empty %}
  <h1>{{ pages.frontpage.title }}</h1>
  <div>{{ pages.frontpage.content }}</div>
{% endunless %}
```

Both empty strings and empty arrays will return *true* if checked for equivalence with *empty*.

Liquid Expressions

The following Liquid expressions are supported:

Common Variables

Workflow Variables

Use the following syntax to access a workflow variable:

```
{{ Variables.NameOfVariable }}
```

For example, given a workflow variable called FIRSTNAME with a value of "Alice", the expression

```
Hello {{ Variables.FirstName }}.
```

will result in

```
Hello Alice.
```

Input

Input values can be accessed using the following syntax:

```
{{ Input }}
```

Activity Output

To access a named activity's output, use the following syntax:

```
{{ Activities.SomeActivityName.Output }}
```

CorrelationId

Returns the correlation ID (if any) of the currently executing workflow.

```
{{ CorrelationId }}
```

WorkflowInstanceId

Returns the workflow instance ID of the currently executing workflow.

```
{{ WorkflowInstanceId }}
```

WorkflowDefinitionId

Returns the workflow definition ID of the currently executing workflow.

```
{{ WorkflowDefinitionId }}
```

WorkflowDefinitionVersion

Returns the workflow definition version of the currently executing workflow.

```
{{ WorkflowDefinitionVersion }}
```

Configuration

Provides access to a .NET configuration value. See Configuration for more details on available configuration items in World of Workflows.

```
{{ Configuration.SomeSection }}
```

As an example, let's say you have the following JSON in appsettings.json:

```
{
  "Elsa": {
    "Smtp": {
      "Host": "localhost",
      "Port": 2525
    }
  }
}
```

You can access the configured Port value using the following expression:

```
{{ Configuration.Elsa.Smtp.Port }}
```

Common Filters

json

json is a liquid filter that renders the specified value as a JSON string.

```
{{ Input | json }}
```

Example output:

```
{
  "SomeDocument": {
    "Title": "About Elsa Workflows"
  }
}
```

base64

A liquid filter that renders the specified value as a bas64 representation. The value is first converted to a string. If the value is an object, array, dictionary or datetime, it is first serialized using JsonConvert.SerializeObject before being encoded as base64.

```
{{ "Some string value" | base64 }}
```

Example output:

U29tZSBzdHJpbmcgdmFsdWU=

Workflow Filters

workflow_definition_id

workflow_definition_id translates the specified workflow name or workflow tag into a workflow ID. This is useful for activities such as **RunWorkflow** which require a workflow ID to run.

Usage:

```
{{ "SomeWorkflowName" | workflow_definition_id }}
{{ "SomeWorkflowTag" | workflow_definition_id: tag }}
```

HTTP Variables

Request

request provides access to various properties on the current HTTP Request object:

```
{{ Request.QueryString }}
{{ Request.ContentType }}
{{ Request.ContentLength }}
{{ Request.Form }}
{{ Request.Protocol }}
{{ Request.Path }}
{{ Request.PathBase }}
{{ Request.Host }}
{{ Request.IsHttps }}
{{ Request.Scheme }}
{{ Request.Method }}
```

HTTP Filters

signal_url

signal_url is a liquid filter that generates a fully-qualified absolute signal URL that will trigger the workflow instance from which this function is invoked.

Example:

```
{{ "MySignal" | signal_url }}
```

Example output:

```
https://localhost:5001/signals/trigger/{some base64 token}
```

Markup

markup is a liquid filter which provides the text as full html rather and htmlencoded data

```
{{"<h1>Hello</h1>" | markup }}
```

JavaScript Primer

This primer will provide you with the essential knowledge needed to use JavaScript in World of Workflows. JavaScript is a powerful and versatile scripting language that can be used to enhance your application's functionality.

Variables

Variables are used to store data. To declare a variable, use the `let` or `const` keyword, followed by the variable name. Use `let` when the value can change and `const` when it should remain constant.

```
let variableName = 'Elsa Workflows';
const constantVariable = 42;
```

Data Types

JavaScript has a few basic data types:

- *String*: Textual data enclosed in single or double quotes.
- *Number*: Numeric data (both integers and floating-point numbers).
- *Boolean*: `true` or `false` values.
- *Object*: A collection of key-value pairs.
- *Array*: An ordered collection of values.
- *Null*: Represents an empty or non-existent value.
- *Undefined*: Represents an uninitialized variable.

Control Structures

Control structures are used to manage the flow of your code. Some common control structures are:

If statement

Executes a block of code if a specified condition is true.

```
if (condition) {
    // Code to be executed
}
```

If-else statement

Executes one block of code if the condition is true, and another block if it is false.

```
if (condition) {
    // Code to be executed if condition is true
} else {
    // Code to be executed if condition is false
}
```

While loop

Executes a block of code as long as the condition is true.

```
while (condition) {
    // Code to be executed
}
```

For loop

Executes a block of code a specific number of times.

```
for (let i = 0; i < count; i++) {
    // Code to be executed
}
```

Functions

Functions are reusable blocks of code that perform a specific task. To define a function, use the `function` keyword, followed by the function name, a list of parameters, and the function body.

```
function functionName(parameter1, parameter2) {
    // Code to be executed
}
```

To call a function, use its name followed by the arguments:

```
functionName(argument1, argument2);
```

Objects and Arrays

Objects store key-value pairs, where each key is associated with a value. To create an object, use the following syntax:

```
const objectName = {
    key1: value1,
    key2: value2,
};
```

Access properties using dot notation or bracket notation:

```
objectName.key1; // value1
objectName['key2']; // value2
```

Arrays store ordered collections of values. To create an array, use the following syntax:

```
const arrayName = [value1, value2, value3];
```

Access values in an array using their index (zero-based):

```
arrayName[0]; // value1
arrayName[1]; // value2
```

Working with Strings

Here are some common string operations:

Concatenation

Combine strings using the `+` operator.

```
let combinedString = 'Hello, ' + 'World!';
```

String interpolation

Embed expressions within a string using template literals.

```
let name = 'Elsa';
let message = `Hello, ${name}!`;
```

String methods

JavaScript provides many built-in string methods to manipulate and work with strings. Here is a list of commonly used string methods:

- *charAt(index):* Returns the character at the specified index.
- *charCodeAt(index):* Returns the Unicode value of the character at the specified index.
- *concat(str1, str2, ...):* Concatenates two or more strings and returns the resulting string.
- *endsWith(searchString, length):* Determines if a string ends with the characters of the specified searchString.
- *includes(searchString, startPosition):* Determines if a string contains the specified searchString.
- *indexOf(searchString, startPosition):* Returns the index of the first occurrence of the specified searchString or -1 if not found.
- *lastIndexOf(searchString, startPosition):* Returns the index of the last occurrence of the specified searchString or -1 if not found.
- *match(regExp):* Searches for a match between a regular expression and a string, and returns the matches.
- *matchAll(regExp):* Returns an iterator of all results matching a regular expression in a string.
- *normalize(form):* Returns the Unicode Normalization Form of the string.
- *padEnd(targetLength, padString):* Pads the end of the string with the specified padString to reach the targetLength.
- *padStart(targetLength, padString):* Pads the start of the string with the specified padString to reach the targetLength.
- *repeat(count):* Repeats the string a specified number of times.
- *replace(searchValue, newValue):* Searches for a specified searchValue and replaces it with a newValue.
- *replaceAll(searchValue, newValue):* Searches for all occurrences of a specified searchValue and replaces them with a newValue.
- *search(regExp):* Searches for a match between a regular expression and a string, and returns the index of the match or -1 if not found.
- *slice(startIndex, endIndex):* Extracts a section of the string and returns it as a new string.
- *split(separator, limit):* Splits a string into an array of substrings using a specified separator.
- *startsWith(searchString, position):* Determines if a string starts with the characters of the specified searchString.
- *substr(startIndex, length):* Returns a part of the string from the specified startIndex with the specified length.
- *substring(startIndex, endIndex):* Returns a part of the string between the specified startIndex and endIndex.

- *toLocaleLowerCase():* Returns the string in lowercase using the host's current locale.
- *toLocaleUpperCase():* Returns the string in uppercase using the host's current locale.
- *toLowerCase():* Returns the string in lowercase.
- *toUpperCase():* Returns the string in uppercase.
- *trim():* Removes whitespace from both ends of a string.
- *trimStart():* Removes whitespace from the beginning of a string.
- *trimEnd():* Removes whitespace from the end of a string.
- *valueOf():* Returns the primitive value of a string object.

These string methods can help you perform various operations on strings, such as searching, replacing, modifying case, splitting, and more. Keep in mind that strings in JavaScript are immutable; these methods return new strings and do not modify the original string.

```
let text = 'World of Workflows';
let lowerCaseText = text.toLowerCase(); // 'world of workflows'
let upperCaseText = text.toUpperCase(); // 'WORLD OF WORKFLOWS'
let position = text.indexOf('Workflows'); // 5
let slicedText = text.slice(0, 5); // 'World'
let replacedText = text.replace('Workflows', 'App'); // 'World of App'
```

Working with Arrays

Here are some common array operations:

push

Add an element to the end of an array using `push()`:

```
let array = [1, 2, 3];
array.push(4); // array becomes [1, 2, 3, 4]
```

pop

Remove the last element from an array using `pop()`:

```
let array = [1, 2, 3];
array.pop(); // array becomes [1, 2]
```

unshift

Add an element to the beginning of an array using `unshift()`:

```
let array = [1, 2, 3];
array.unshift(0); // array becomes [0, 1, 2, 3]
```

shift

Remove the first element from an array using `shift()`:

```
let array = [1, 2, 3];
array.shift(); // array becomes [2, 3]
```

forEach

Iterate through the elements of an array using a `for` loop or the `forEach()` method:

```
let array = [1, 2, 3];

// Using a for loop
for (let i = 0; i < array.length; i++) {
    console.log(array[i]); // 1, 2, 3
}

// Using forEach()
array.forEach((element) => {
    console.log(element); // 1, 2, 3
});
```

Error Handling

To handle errors in JavaScript, you can use the `try...catch` statement:

```
try {
    // Code that might throw an error
} catch (error) {
    // Code to handle the error
}
```

For example, if you want to handle an error when parsing JSON data:

```
let jsonData = '{ "name": "Workflows"';

try {
    let obj = JSON.parse(jsonData);
    console.log(obj.name); // 'Workflows'
} catch (error) {
    console.error('An error occurred:', error.message); // 'An
error occurred: Unexpected end of JSON input'
}
```

This JavaScript primer should help you get started with using JavaScript in your Elsa Workflows application. As you continue to develop your application, you can explore more advanced concepts and techniques, as well as integrate external libraries and APIs to further enhance its capabilities.

JavaScript in World of Workflows

The following JavaScript expressions are supported:

Variables

Workflow Variables

Any workflow *variable* can be accessed directly as if they were a global variable.

For example, if the **SETVARIABLE** activity sets a variable called *FirstName* to 'Luke', it can be accessed as follows:

```
`Hello ${FirstName}`
```

Value stored in the variable:

```
"Hello Luke"
```

This also works when setting variables using the *setVariable()* function. Because ultimately, both the *SetVariable* activity and *setVariable()* function use the same API under the cover to set a workflow variable.

Activity Output

A activity might provide some output which can then be accessed from any other activity using workflow expressions.

For example, to access an activity's output property called **OUTPUT** using a JavaScript expression, you can do so by specifying *activities*, then the activity name followed by *.Output()*. Notice that you must invoke the property as if it were a method (i.e. using *()* at the end). This is due to the way workflow storage providers work, which are potentially asynchronous in nature (such as Azure Blob Storage).

For example, if you have an activity named *MyActivity*, you can access its output as follows:

```
activities.MyActivity.Output().
```

If the output is an object, you can access its properties too. For instance, the HTTP Endpoint activity returns the HTTP request as its output which is of type **HTTPREQUESTMODEL**. When you name this activity *MyHttpEndpoint*, you can access the HTTP request *Body* like this:

```
activities.MyHttpEndpoint.Output().Body
```

If you happened to post a JSON document to your HTTP endpoint that looks like this:

```
{
  "MyDocument": {
    "Title": "About Elsa Workflows"
  }
}
```

Then you can access the *Title* field like this:

```
activities.MyHttpEndpoint.Output().Body.MyDocument.Title
```

If your activity is a direct child of an HTTP Endpoint activity, you can access its output directly via the *input* variable, which will be an instance of **HTTPREQUESTMODEL**.

input

Contains the *input* value that was received as *output* from the previously executed activity, if any.

```
input: object?
```

workflowInstanceId

Contains the workflow instance ID of the currently executing workflow.

```
workflowInstanceId: string
```

workflowDefinitionId

Contains the workflow definition ID of the currently executing workflow.

```
workflowDefinitionId: string
```

workflowDefinitionVersion

Contains the workflow definition version of the currently executing workflow.

```
workflowDefinitionVersion: number
```

correlationId

Contains the correlation ID of the currently executing workflow.

```
correlationId: string?
```

currentCulture

Contains the current culture.

```
currentCulture: CultureInfo
```

Currently, this value is always set to CultureInfo.InvariantCulture.

workflowContext

Contains the workflow context (if any) of the currently executing workflow.

```
workflowContext: object?
```

Common Functions

guid

Generates a new GUID value and returns its string representation.

```
guid(): string
```

This function is a thin wrapper around the following .NET code:

```
Guid.NewGuid().ToString().
```

parseGuid

Parses a string into a GUID value.

```
parseGuid(value: string): Guid
```

This function is a thin wrapper around the following .NET code:

```
Guid.Parse(value).
```

setVariable

Sets a workflow variable to the specified value.

```
setVariable(name: string, value: object): void
```

This function is a thin wrapper around the following .NET code:

```
activityContext.SetVariable(name, value).
```

getVariable

Returns a workflow variable with the specified name.

```
getVariable(name: string): object
```

Instead of using getVariable(name: string), you can access workflow variables directly as described above in the Workflow Variables section.

This function is a thin wrapper around the following .NET code:

```
activityContext.GetVariable(name).
```

getConfig

Provides access to a .NET configuration value.

```
getConfig(name: string): string
```

As an example, let's say you have the following JSON in appsettings.json:

```
{
  "Elsa": {
    "Smtp": {
      "Host": "localhost",
      "Port": 2525
    }
  }
}
```

You can access the configured Port value using the following expression:

```
getConfig("Elsa:Smtp:Port") // returns '2525'
```
This function is a thin wrapper around the following .NET code:
```
configuration.GetSection(name).Value
```
where configuration is an instance of IConfiguration.

isNullOrWhiteSpace

Returns true if the specified string is null, empty or consists of white space only, false otherwise.

```
isNullOrWhiteSpace(value: string): boolean
```

This function is a thin wrapper around the following .NET code:
```
string.IsNullOrWhiteSpace(value).
```

isNullOrEmpty

Returns true if the specified string is null or empty, false otherwise.

```
isNullOrEmpty(value: string): boolean
```

This function is a thin wrapper around the following .NET code:
```
string.IsNullOrEmpty(value).
```

Workflow Functions

getWorkflowDefinitionIdByName

Returns the ID of the specified workflow by name. This is useful when for instance you are using the **RUNWORKFLOW** activity, which requires the ID of the workflow definition to run.

```
getWorkflowDefinitionIdByName(name: string): string?
```

For example: set the *Workflow Definition* in a **RUNWORKFLOW** activity to *MyWorkflow* :

```
getWorkflowDefinitionIdByName('MyWorkflow')
```

getWorkflowDefinitionIdByTag

Returns the ID of the specified workflow by tag. This is useful when for instance you are using the **RUNWORKFLOW** activity, which requires the ID of the workflow definition to run.

```
getWorkflowDefinitionIdByTag(tag: string): string?
```

HTTP Functions

queryString

Returns the value of the specified query string parameter.

```
queryString(name: string): string
```

absoluteUrl

Converts the specified relative path into a fully-qualified absolute URL.

```
absoluteUrl(path: string): string
```

signalUrl

Generates a fully-qualified absolute signal URL that will trigger the workflow instance from which this function is invoked.

signalUrl(signal: string): string

Date/Time Functions

instantFromDateTimeUtc

Returns a new Instant object from the specified DateTime value.

Make sure that the DateTime value's Kind property is DateTimeKind.Utc.

currentInstant

Returns the current date/time value in the form of a NodaTime's Instant object.

currentInstant(): Instant

currentYear

Returns the current year.

currentYear(): number

startOfMonth

Returns the start of the month of the specified instant. If no instant is specified, the current instant is used.

startOfMonth(instant: Instant?): LocalDate;

endOfMonth(instant: Instant?)

Returns the end of the month of the specified instant. If no instant is specified, the current instant is used.

endOfMonth(instant: Instant?): LocalDate;

startOfPreviousMonth

Returns the start of the previous month of the specified instant. If no instant is specified, the current instant is used.

```
startOfPreviousMonth(instant: Instant?): LocalDate;
```

plus

Adds the specified Duration to the specified Instant and returns the result.

```
plus(instant: Instant, duration: Duration): Instant
```

minus

Subtracts the specified Duration from the specified Instant and returns the result.

```
minus(instant: Instant, duration: Duration): Instant
```

durationFromDays

Returns a duration constructed from the specified number of days.

```
durationFromDays(days: number): Duration
```

formatInstant

Formats the specified Instant using the specified format string and CultureInfo. If no culture info is provided, CultureInfo.InvariantCulture is used.

```
formatInstant(instant: Instant, format: string, cultureInfo:
CultureInfo?): string
```

localDateFromInstant

Returns the LocalDate portion of the specified Instant.

```
localDateFromInstant(instant: Instant): LocalDate
```

instantFromLocalDate

Creates an Instant from the specified LocalDate value (start of date).

```
instantFromLocalDate(localDate: LocalDate): Instant
```

Plugins

Plugins extend the capability of World of Workflows by adding capabilities to the system. At time of printing, the following plugins were available:

- **AutoTask** – access and work with data and objects in the AutoTask PSA application
- **Azure** – Manipulate and manage Microsoft Azure environments
- **OpenAI** – Work with services from OpenAI, including ChatGPT, GPT4, DALL-E, Whisper and more
- **Office 365** – Work with Microsoft Office 365 and the Microsoft Graph API
- **Xero** – Work with the Xero cloud based accounting system
- **Utilities** – Various utilities to extend world of workflows